The Question of Happiness

The Question of Happiness

✦

On Finding Meaning, Pleasure, and the Ultimate Currency

Tal Ben-Shahar

Writers Club Press
San Jose New York Lincoln Shanghai

The Question of Happiness
On Finding Meaning, Pleasure, and the Ultimate Currency

Writers Club Press
an imprint of iUniverse, Inc.

For information address:
iUniverse, Inc.
5220 S. 16th St., Suite 200
Lincoln, NE 68512
www.iuniverse.com

ISBN: 0-595-23140-3

Printed in the United States of America

To my family

Contents

Acknowledgements

For the last three years Kim Cooper has been my writing teacher, editor, and—above all—dear friend. When I first showed Kim a manuscript of this book I expected a few minor recommendations before I could send it off to publishers. It was not to be. The hundreds of hours we subsequently spent dissecting and putting back together each and every idea, sentence, and word—arguing, discussing, sharing, laughing—have made writing this book the labor of happiness.

I wrote this book with much help from friends, students, and teachers. My special thanks to Johan Berman, Nathaniel Branden, Sandra Cha, I-Jin Chew, Leemore Dafny, Margot and Udi Eiran, Liat and Shai Feinberg, Dave Fish, Shayne Fitz-Coy, Adam Grant, Richard Hackman, Nat Harrison, Anne Hwang, Ohad Kamin, Joe Kaplan, Ellen Langer, Maren Lau, Pat Lee, Brian Little, Joshua Margolis, Dan Markel, Bonnie Masland, Sasha Mattu, Jamie Miller, Mihnea Moldoveanu, Damian Moskovitz, Ronen Nakash, Josephine Pichanick, Samuel Rascoff, Shannon Ringvelski, Amir Rubin, Philip Stone, and Pavel Vasilyev.

In leisurely conversations and through their participation in work-shops, colleagues and friends from Tanker Pacific have played an important role in the formulation of the ideas in this book.

I have been blessed with a large and close-knit family—they create a circle of happiness for me. To the Ben-Shahars, Ben-Poraths, Grobers, Kolodnys, Markses, my gratitude for the countless hours we spent—and will continue to spend—discussing and living the good life. To my grand-parents, for living through the worst and exemplifying the best.

Many of the ideas in this book have emerged from discussions with my brother and sister, Zeev and Aterett, two brilliant and insightful psychologists. Tami, my wife and help meet, patiently listens to my ideas when they are in the raw, and then reads, criticizes, and comments on everything that I write. My parents provided me the foundation from which I was able to write about, and more importantly find, happiness.

Introduction

The Question of Happiness

In the middle of difficulty lies opportunity.

—Albert Einstein

I was sixteen years old when I won the Israeli national squash championship. It was an event that brought the subject of happiness into sharp focus in my life.

I had always believed that winning the title would make me happy, would alleviate the emptiness I felt so much of the time. For the five years I had trained for the event I felt that something important was missing from my life—something that all of the miles run, the weights lifted, the self-motivating speeches playing and replaying in my mind, were not providing. I was unhappy, but believed that it was a matter of time before that "missing something" would find its way into my life. After all, it seemed clear to me that the mental and physical exertion were necessary to win the championship. Winning the championship was necessary for fulfillment. Fulfillment was necessary for happiness. That was the logic I operated under.

And, in fact, when I won the Israeli Nationals, I was ecstatic, happier than I had ever imagined myself being. Following the final match I went out with my family and friends, and we celebrated together. I was certain then, that the belief that had carried me through the five years of preparation—that winning the title would make me happy—was justified; the hard work, the physical and emotional pain, had paid off.

After the night of celebration, I retired to my room. I sat on my bed and wanted to savor, for the last time before going to sleep, that feeling of supreme happiness. Suddenly, without warning, the bliss that came from having attained in real life what had for so long been my most cherished and exalted fantasy disappeared, and my feeling of emptiness returned. I was befuddled, and afraid. The tears of joy shed only hours earlier turned to tears of pain and helplessness. For if I was not happy now, when everything seemed to have worked out perfectly, what prospects did I have of attaining lasting happiness?

I tried to convince myself that I was feeling the temporary low following an overwhelming high. But as the days and months unfolded I did not feel happier; in fact, I was growing even more desolate as I began to see that simply substituting a new goal—winning the world championship, say—would not in itself lead me to happiness. There no longer seemed to be a series of logical steps for me to follow.

I realized that I needed to think about happiness in different ways, to deepen or change my understanding of the nature of happiness. I became obsessed with the answer to a single question: How can I find lasting happiness? I pursued it fervently—I observed people who seemed happy and asked what it was that made them happy; I read everything I could find on the topic of happiness, from Aristotle to Confucius, from ancient philosophy to modern psychology, from academic research to self-help books.

To continue my exploration of the question of happiness in a more formal way, I decided to study philosophy and psychology in college. I met brilliant people who had dedicated themselves as writers, thinkers, artists, teachers, to understanding the "big questions." Learning to read a text closely and analytically, attending lectures on intrinsic motivation and on creativity, reading Plato on "the good" and Emerson on "the integrity of your own mind"—all of these provided me with new lenses through which my life and the lives of those around me came into clearer focus.

I realized that I was not alone in my unhappiness: many of my classmates seemed to be dispirited and stressed. And yet, I was struck by how little time they dedicated to what I believed to be the question of questions. They spent their time pursuing high grades, athletic achievements, and prestigious jobs, but the pursuit—and attainment—of these goals failed to provide them with an experience of sustained well-being.

Although their specific goals changed when they left college (promotion at work replacing academic success, for instance), the essential pattern of their lives remained the same. So many people seemed to accept their poor emotional predicament as the inevitable price of success. Could it be, then, that Thoreau's observation, that most people lead lives of "quiet desperation," was true? Even if it was, I refused to accept his dire assessment as a necessary fact of life, and sought answers to the following questions: How could we be both successful and happy? How could ambition and happiness be reconciled? Is it possible to defy the maxim of no pain, no gain?

In trying to answer these questions I realized that I would first have to figure out what happiness is. Is it an emotion? Is it the same as pleasure? Is it the absence of pain? The experience of bliss? Words like *pleasure*, *bliss*, *ecstasy*, and *contentment* are often used interchangeably with the word *happiness*, but none of them describes precisely what I mean when I think about happiness. These emotions are fleeting, and while they are enjoyable and significant, they are not the measure—or the pillars—of happiness. We can experience sadness at times and still enjoy overall happiness.

While it was clear to me which words and definitions were inadequate, finding those that could capture the nature of happiness proved more difficult. We all talk about happiness and mostly know it when we experience it, but we lack a coherent definition that can help us identify its antecedents. The source of the word "happiness" is the Icelandic word *happ* which means "luck" or "chance," the same source of the words *haphazard* and *happenstance*. I did not want to leave the experience of happiness to chance, and therefore sought to define and understand it. This book is my attempt to do so.

I do not have the complete answer to the single question I posed at sixteen—I suspect that I will never have it. Through my reading, research, observation and reflection, I have discovered no secret formula, no "five easy steps to happiness." My objective in writing this book is to raise awareness of the general principles underlying a happy and fulfilling life.

◆   ◆   ◆

In this book, I approach the question of happiness from a philosophical, as well as psychological, perspective. Within psychology, I limit my discussion to "Positive Psychology," an area of the field dealing with happiness, virtue, well-being, and self-esteem. The book does not attempt, nor does it pretend, to address the many obstacles to leading a fulfilling life—internal obstacles such as clinical depression or extreme neurosis, external obstacles such as poverty or political oppression.

I have divided the book into three sections. In the first part, Chapters 1 through 3, I discuss what happiness is and the essential components of a happy life; in the second part, Chapters 4 through 6, I focus on putting these ideas into practice in education, in the workplace, and in relationships; the third part comprises four meditations in which I offer some final thoughts on the nature of happiness and on its place in our lives.

In Chapter 1, I present the Happiness Model and argue that happiness arises neither from simply satisfying immediate desires, nor from the infinite delay of satisfaction. Our usual models for happiness—the hedonist who lives only for pleasure in the moment, and the rat racer who postpones gratification for the purpose of attaining some future goal—do not work for most people, because they ignore our basic need for a sense of both present and future benefit.

In Chapter 2, I demonstrate why in order to be happy we need to find both meaning and pleasure—to have both a sense of purpose and the experience of positive emotions. Happiness, I argue, should be held as the ultimate human end, the end toward which all other ends lead.

In Chapter 3, I suggest that happiness, not money or prestige, should be regarded as the ultimate currency—the currency by which we take measure of our lives. I consider the relationship between material wealth and happiness and ask why so many people are in danger of emotional bankruptcy despite unprecedented levels of material wealth.

In Chapter 4, I begin to apply the theory presented in Part I of the book and ask why most students dislike school, and look at ways in which educators—parents and teachers—can help students to be both happy *and* successful. I introduce two radically different approaches toward the process of learning: the drowning model and the lovemaking model.

In Chapter 5, I question the prevalent assumption that a trade-off between an intrinsic sense of fulfillment and extrinsic success at work is inevitable. I discuss the process by which we can identify work that we find meaningful and pleasurable, and that we are good at.

In Chapter 6, I consider one of the most significant elements of a happy life: relationships. I talk about what it *really* means to love and be loved unconditionally; why this kind of love is essential for a happy relationship; and how it can contribute to the experience of pleasure and meaning in other areas of our lives.

In the first meditation of the final part of the book, I discuss the relationship among happiness, self-interest, and benevolence. In the second meditation I argue against the idea that our level of happiness is predetermined by our genetic makeup or early experiences, and cannot be changed. The third meditation identifies some of the psychological barriers—internal limitations we impose upon ourselves—that stand in the way of living a fulfilling life, barriers that can be overcome by recognizing our birthright to be happy. The fourth meditation provides a thought experiment that offers a point from which we can reflect upon, and find some answers to, the question of questions.

William of Occam, a thirteenth-century English philosopher, argued that, in coming up with a theory, we have to make things as simple as they can be and as complex as they have to be. The ideas in this small book are fairly simple; this does not, however, make them easy to implement. The hardest part, living in accordance with these principles, is the responsibility—and privilege—of each individual.

PART I

What Is Happiness?

Chapter 1

The Happiness Model

○ ○

Nature has given the opportunity of happiness to all, knew they but how to use it.

—Claudian

One of the most important squash tournaments of the year was approaching. I had been training extremely hard and decided to supplement my training with a special diet. While my eating habits had always been quite healthful—a necessary part of my training regimen—I had occasionally allowed myself the "luxury" of junk food.

However, in the month leading up to the tournament I ate only the leanest fish and chicken, whole-grain carbohydrates, and fresh fruit and vegetables. The reward for my abstinence, I resolved, would be a two-day junk-food binge.

As soon as the tournament was over, I went straight to my favorite hamburger joint. I ordered four hamburgers, and as I walked away from the counter with my prize, I understood how Pavlov's dogs felt at the sound of the bell. I sat myself down and hurriedly unwrapped the first portion of my reward, but as I brought the burger closer to my mouth, I stopped.

I did not want to eat the burger. For four weeks I had looked forward to this meal, and now, when it was right in front of me, presented to me on a plastic platter, I did not want it. I tried to figure out why, and it was then that I came up with the Happiness Model, otherwise known as *The Hamburger Model.*

I realized that in the month I had been eating well, my body felt cleansed and I was surging with energy. I knew that I would enjoy eating the four burgers, but that afterward I would feel unpleasant and fatigued.

Staring at my untouched meal, I thought of four kinds of hamburgers, each representing a distinct archetype, with each archetype describing a distinct pattern of attitudes and behaviors.

The first archetypal hamburger is the one I had just turned down, the tasty "junk-food" burger. Eating this hamburger would yield *present benefit* in that I would enjoy it, and *future detriment* in that I would subsequently feel unwell.

The experience of present benefit and future detriment defines the *hedonism* archetype. The hedonist lives by the maxim "seek pleasure and avoid pain"; she focuses on enjoying the present while ignoring the potential negative consequences of her actions.

The second hamburger type that came to mind was a tasteless vegetarian burger made with only the most healthful ingredients, which would afford me *future benefit* in that I would subsequently feel good and healthy, and *present detriment* in that I would not enjoy eating it.

The corresponding archetype is that of the *rat race*. The rat racer, subordinating the present to the future, suffers now for the purpose of some anticipated gain.

The third hamburger type, the worst of all possible burgers, is both tasteless and unhealthful: eating it, I would experience *present detriment* in that it tastes bad, and suffer *future detriment*, in that it is unhealthful.

The parallel to this burger is the archetype of *resignation* or *learned helplessness*. This archetype describes the behavior of a person who has lost his lust for life; he neither enjoys the moment, nor does he have a sense of future purpose.

The three archetypes that I came up with did not exhaust all possibilities—there was one more to consider. What about a hamburger that would be as tasty as the one I had turned down and as healthy as the vegetarian burger? A burger that would constitute a complete experience with both present and future benefit?

This hamburger exemplifies the *happiness* archetype. A happy person lives secure in the knowledge that the activities that bring her enjoyment in the present will also lead to a fulfilling future.

The following graph illustrates the relationship between present and future benefit in the four archetypes. The vertical axis represents the future dimension of the experience with *future benefit* on the positive side and *future detriment* on the negative side. The horizontal axis of the graph represents the present dimension of the experience with *present benefit* on the positive side and *present detriment* on the negative side.

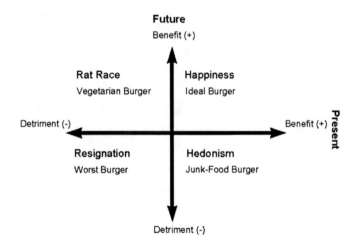

The archetypes, as I present them, are theoretical formulations of *types*, not of actual people. To varying degrees, and in different combinations, we all have characteristics of the rat racer, the hedonist, the person who is resigned, and the one who is happy. For the purpose of clarifying the essential characteristics, my descriptions will be like caricatures—resembling actual people, but with the distinguishing characteristics accentuated. To exemplify the archetypes we will follow the life of Timon, an imaginary character.

The Rat-Race Archetype

As a young child, Timon is unconcerned with the future, experiencing the wonder and excitement of his day-to-day activities. When he turns six and goes to school his career as a rat racer begins.

He is constantly reminded by his parents and teachers that the purpose of going to school is to get good grades so that he can secure his future. He is *not* told that he should be happy in school or that learning can be—and ought to be—fun.

Afraid of performing poorly on tests, fearful of missing a word of the teacher's gospel, Timon feels anxious and stressed. He looks forward to the end of each period and each day, and is only sustained by the thought of the upcoming holiday when he will no longer have to think about work and grades.

Timon accepts the values of the adults—that grades are the measure of success—and despite the fact that he dislikes school, he continues to work hard. When he does well, his parents and teachers compliment him, and his classmates—who, too, have been indoctrinated—envy him. By the time he enters high school, Timon has fully internalized the formula for success: sacrifice present enjoyment in order to be happy in the future; no pain, no gain. Although he does not enjoy his schoolwork or his extracurricular activities, he devotes himself fully to them. He is driven by the need to amass titles and honors, and when the pressure becomes overwhelming, he tells himself that he will begin to have fun once he gets into college.

Timon applies to college and gets into the school of his choice. He cries as he reads the acceptance letter, joyful and relieved. Now, he tells himself, he can finally be happy.

The relief is short-lived, however. A few days go by and Timon is again gripped by the same sense of anxiety he has been feeling for years. He fears that he will not be able to compete with the best students in the college, the academic elite. And if he cannot, how will he get the job he wants?

His rat race continues. Through his four years of college he works at building an impressive résumé: forming a student organization, becoming president of another, volunteering in a homeless shelter, and playing varsity athletics. He chooses courses carefully—enrolling in them not because they excite him, but because they will look good on his transcript.

Timon does have a good time every now and then, especially after handing in a paper or exam. These good moments, which come from being relieved of a burden, are short-lived; his work builds up again—and along with it, his anxiety.

In the spring of his senior year, Timon receives a job offer from a prestigious firm. He happily accepts it. Now, he thinks, he will finally be able to enjoy his life. Soon, however, he realizes that he does *not* enjoy his eighty-hour-per-week job. He tells himself, once more, that he must sacrifice for the time being, just until he is established and secure in his career. Once in a while, he feels good—when he receives a raise, a large bonus, or a promotion. The sense of fulfillment disappears, though, as drudgery returns.

After years of hard work, he is offered a partnership in the firm. He vaguely remembers thinking that he would be content if he became a partner—but he is not.

Timon was a top student in college; he is a partner in a prestigious firm; he has a large house in the best neighborhood; he drives a luxury car; he has more money than he can spend. Timon is unhappy.

Yet, others regard him as the archetype of success; parents see him as a role model, telling their children that if they work hard, they can be like Timon. He pities those children but cannot imagine what alternatives there are to the rat race. He does not even know what to tell his children:

Not to work hard in school? Not to get into a good college? Not to get a good job? Is being successful synonymous with being miserable?

While Timon is an unhappy rat racer, it is important to note that there are many businessmen and women who are passionate about their work and love to spend eighty hours each week on the job. Being a hard worker, or a high achiever, is not synonymous with being a rat racer; there are supremely happy people who work long hours and dedicate themselves to their schoolwork or to their profession. What differentiates rat racers is their inability to enjoy what they are doing—and their delusion that once they reach a certain destination, they will be happy.

Moreover, in using Timon as an example, I am not suggesting that businesspeople alone are potential rat racers. A person pursuing a career in medicine may share the same attitudes and exhibit the same behavior, feeling pressured to get into a top medical school, then to find a good internship, then to become the head of the department, and so on. The same could apply to a person working in a factory. He exhausts himself working extra shifts so that one day he will be promoted to foreman; then, he believes, he will finally have the luxury to relax and spend more time with his family. By the time he becomes foreman, though, he has already set his sights on the floor manager's job, and so on, and so on.

The reason why we see so many rat racers around is that our culture reinforces this delusional state. If we get an "A" at the end of the semester, we get a gift from our parents; if we meet certain quotas on the job, we get a bonus at the end of the year. We learn to focus on the next goal rather than on our present experience, and chase the ever-elusive future our entire lives. We are not rewarded for enjoying the journey itself, but for the successful *completion* of a journey. Society rewards arrivals, not processes; destinations, not journeys.

Once we arrive at our destination, once we attain our goals, we mistake the relief that we feel for happiness. The weightier the burden we carried on our journey, the more powerful and pleasant is our experience of relief.

When we mistake these moments of relief for happiness we reinforce the *illusion* that simply reaching goals will make us happy.

We can consider the experience of relief to be *negative happiness* as it stems from the negation of stress or anxiety. By its very nature, relief presupposes an unpleasant experience and cannot, therefore, yield lasting happiness. A person who is relieved of a splitting headache will feel happy that she is free of pain—but because that "happiness" had to be preceded by suffering, the absence of pain is but a momentary relief from an essentially negative experience.

The experience of relief is also temporary. When the throbbing in our head goes away, we derive a certain pleasure from the absence of pain, but then very quickly adapt and take our physical contentment for granted.

The rat racer, confusing relief with happiness, continues to chase after his goals, as though simply attaining them will be enough to make him happy.

The Hedonism Archetype

A hedonist seeks pleasure and avoids pain. She goes about satisfying her desires, giving little or no thought to future consequences. A fulfilling life, she believes, is reducible to a succession of pleasurable experiences. That something feels good in the moment is sufficient justification for doing it until the next desire replaces it. She initiates friendships and romances with enthusiasm, but when their novelty wears off, she quickly moves on to the next relationship. Because the hedonist focuses only on the present, she will do things that are potentially detrimental if they afford her immediate gratification. If drugs produce a pleasant experience, she takes them; if she finds work difficult, she avoids it.

The hedonist errs in equating effort with pain, and pleasure with happiness. The gravity of this error is revealed in an old episode of *The Twilight Zone* in which a ruthless criminal, killed while running from the police, is greeted by an angel sent to grant his every wish. The man, fully aware of his life of crime, cannot believe that he is in heaven. He is initially baffled, but then accepts his good fortune and begins to list his desires: he asks for an inordinate sum of money and receives it; he asks for his favorite food and it is served to him; he asks for beautiful women and they appear. Life (after death), it seems, could not be better.

However, as time goes by, the pleasure he derives from continuous indulgence begins to diminish; the effortlessness of his existence becomes tiresome. He asks the angel for some work that will challenge him and is told that in this place he can get whatever he wants—except the chance to work for the things he receives.

Without any challenges, the criminal becomes increasingly frustrated. Finally, in utter desperation, he says to the angel that he wants to get out, to go to "the other place." The criminal, assuming that he is in heaven, wants to go to hell. The camera zooms in on the angel as his delicate face turns devious and threatening. With the ominous laughter of the devil he says, "This is the other place."

This is the hell that the hedonist mistakes for heaven. Without a long-term purpose, devoid of challenge, life ceases to feel meaningful to us; we cannot find happiness if, like animals, we exclusively seek pleasure and avoid pain. Yet the ever-present hedonist within each of us—longing for a Garden of Eden of sorts—equates effort with pain and doing nothing with pleasure.

In 1996, I conducted a leadership seminar for a group of South African executives who had been involved in the struggle against apartheid. They told me that, while fighting against apartheid, they had a clear sense of purpose, a clear future goal—life was exciting and challenging.

When apartheid was abolished, celebrations went on for months. As the euphoria waned, though, many people who had been involved in the struggle began to experience boredom, emptiness, even depression. Of course, they did not wish to return to the days when they were an oppressed majority, but in the absence of the cause to which they had dedicated themselves so fully, they felt a void. Some managed to find a sense of purpose in their family lives, in helping their community, in their work, or in their hobbies; others, years later, are still struggling to find a sense of direction.

Let us now return to Timon, who, having failed to attain happiness by chasing one future goal after another, decides to focus on the present. He indulges in more drinking and drugs, and engages in purely hedonistic relationships. He takes long breaks from work, spends hours sunbathing, enjoying the bliss of purposelessness, of not having to think about tomorrow. For a while, he believes that he is happy, but like the criminal in *The Twilight Zone*, Timon quickly becomes bored.

The Resignation Archetype

If the rat-race archetype describes the state of living for the future and the hedonism archetype the state of living for the present, then the resignation archetype captures the state of being chained to the past. People who live resigned to their present unhappiness, and look forward to the same sort of life in the future, are fettered to their past failures to attain happiness.

Such attachment to past failures has been described by the psychologist Martin Seligman as "learned helplessness." To study this phenomenon, Seligman placed dogs in three experimental groups. The dogs in the first group were given mild electric shocks, which they could turn off by pressing a panel. Dogs in the second group were given shocks that persisted regardless of their actions. The third group of dogs, the control group, received no shocks.

All the dogs were later put in boxes from which they could escape by jumping over a low barrier, and were then given electric shocks. The dogs in the first group (who had been able to stop the shocks earlier) and the dogs from the third group (who had not previously received any shocks) quickly jumped over the barrier and escaped. The dogs in the second group, who could not prevent the electric shocks earlier, made no effort to escape. They simply lay down in the box and whimpered while receiving shocks. These dogs had learned to be helpless.

In a similar experiment, Seligman subjected people to a loud and unpleasant noise. In one group, people were able to control the noise, to stop it, whereas people in the second group could not. Later, when both groups were subjected to loud noise that they could have turned off if they had tried, those in the second group did not try—they had resigned themselves to their predicament.

Seligman's work reveals how easily we can learn to be helpless. When we fail to attain a desired outcome, we often extrapolate from that experience the belief that we have no control over our lives or over certain parts of it. Such thinking leads to despair.

Timon, unhappy as a rat racer, equally unhappy as a hedonist, and aware of no other options, resigns himself to unhappiness. What of his children, though? He does not want them to lead lives of "quiet desperation," but he has no idea how to guide them. Should he teach them to bear suffering in the present to attain their goals? How can he when he knows the misery of the rat racer? Should he teach them to live simply for today? He cannot, because he knows too well the hollowness of the hedonistic life.

The Happiness Archetype

One of my students at Harvard came to talk to me after receiving a job offer from a prestigious consulting firm. She told me that she was uninterested in the work she would be doing but felt she could not turn down this opportunity. She had had offers from many other companies, some for jobs that she would enjoy much more, but none that would "set her up" as well as this one. She asked me at what point in life—at what age—she could stop thinking about the future and start being happy.

I did not accept her question with its implicit either/or approach to happiness. I told her that instead of asking "Should I be happy now *or* in the future?" she should ask, "How can I be happy now *and* in the future?"

While present and future benefit may sometimes conflict—because some situations demand that we forgo one for the other—it is possible to enjoy both. Students who truly love learning, for instance, derive present benefit from the pleasure they take in discovering new ideas *and* future benefit from the ways in which those ideas will prepare them for their careers. In romantic relationships, some couples enjoy their time together *and* help each other grow and develop. Those who enjoy present and future benefit demonstrate that happiness—like the healthy and tasty hamburger—is attainable.

To expect *constant* happiness, though, is to set ourselves up for failure and disappointment. Not everything that we do can provide us both present and future benefit. It is sometimes worthwhile to forgo present benefit for greater future gain, and in every life some mundane work is unavoidable. Studying for exams or saving for the future is often unpleasant, but can help us to attain long-term happiness.

Living as a hedonist, every now and then, has its benefits as well. As long as there are no long-term negative consequences (such as from the use of drugs), focusing solely on the present can rejuvenate us. In moderation, the relaxation, the mindlessness, the fun, that come from lying on the beach or watching television, can make us happier.

Reconciling Future and Present

Robert M. Pirsig in *Zen and the Art of Motorcycle Maintenance*, describes how he joined a group of elderly Zen monks mountain-climbing in the Himalayas. Though Pirsig was the youngest member of the expedition, he was the only one who struggled; he eventually gave up while the monks effortlessly ascended to the peak.

Pirsig, focused on reaching the peak of the mountain, and overwhelmed by what still lay ahead, was unable to enjoy the climb; he lost his desire—and his strength—to carry on. The monks also focused on the peak, but only to make sure they were staying on course, not because reaching the peak itself was most important to them. Knowing that they were headed in the right direction allowed them to focus their attention and enjoy each step, rather than being overwhelmed by what still lay ahead.

The proper role of long-term goals is to *liberate* us, so that we can enjoy the here and now. If we set off on a road trip without any identified destination, the trip itself will not be much fun. If we do not know where we are going or even where we want to go, every fork in the road becomes a site of ambivalence—neither turning left nor turning right seems a good choice as we do not know whether we want to end up where these roads lead. So instead of focusing on the landscape, the scenery, the flowers on the side of the road, we are consumed by hesitation and uncertainty. What will happen if I go this way? Where will I end up if I turn here? If we have a destination in mind, if we more or less know where we are going, we are free to focus our full attention on making the most of where we *are*.

The emphasis in my theory is not so much on *attaining* long-term goals as it is on *having* them. The primary purpose of having long-term goals is to facilitate the enjoyment of the present. *Long-term goals are means, not just ends.*

While attaining a sought after goal can provide much satisfaction, and the failure to attain a certain goal can lead to despair, these feelings tend to be short-lived. Psychologist Philip Brickman and his colleagues demonstrated that within as short a period as a month lottery winners return to their base levels of well-being—if they were unhappy before winning, they will remain so. The psychologist Daniel Gilbert extended these findings to show how, in general, we fail to predict our future affective states. For example, professors who are up for tenure predict that getting tenure (or not) will have a significant and lasting influence on their emotional well-being, but, in fact, after a brief period of time their levels of happiness return to where they were before they received the verdict—whether they get tenure or not.

In most cases, attaining a goal (or failing to) produces only temporary fluctuations in our base level of happiness. Yet we continue to believe—and act upon the belief—that reaching some destination will lead to lasting happiness.

◆   ◆   ◆

The rat racer's illusion is that reaching the destination will bring him happiness; he does not recognize the significance of the journey. The hedonist's illusion is that only the journey is important. The resigned person, having given up on both the destination and the journey, is disillusioned with life. The rat racer becomes a slave to the future; the hedonist, a slave to the moment; the resigned person, a slave to the past.

Attaining lasting happiness requires that we enjoy the *journey* on our way toward a *destination* we deem valuable. Happiness is not about making it to the peak of the mountain, nor is it about climbing aimlessly around the mountain; *happiness is the experience of climbing toward the peak.*

Chapter 2

Happiness Explained

Happiness is the meaning and the purpose of life, the whole aim and end of human existence.

—Aristotle

Why Pursue Happiness?

We are all familiar with children's insatiable curiosity. Why does it rain? Why does water rise to the sky? Why does water become gas? Why do the clouds not fall? Whether or not children get actual answers to their questions is of little relevance. Once they begin to question a certain phenomenon in the wonder-filled world around them, they do not relent. Their relentless probing follows the pattern of "the infinitely regressive why"—regardless of the answer to a question, the child persists with another "Why?"

However, one question allows an adult to end the onslaught of "whys" without any feelings of guilt or inadequacy. This question is: "Why do you want to be happy?" When questioning why we want certain things, other than happiness, we can always question their value with another "Why?" For example, why are you training so hard? Why do you want to win the championship? Why do you want to be rich and famous? Why do you want a fancy car, a mansion, a yacht?

When the question is "Why do you want to be happy?" the answer is simple and definitive. We pursue happiness because it is in our nature as human beings to do so. When the answer to a question is "Because it will make me happy," nothing can challenge the validity and finality of the answer. Happiness is the highest on the hierarchy of goals, the end toward which all other ends lead.

The British Philosopher David Hume argues that, "The great end of all human industry is the attainment of happiness. For this were arts invented, sciences cultivated, laws ordained, and societies modeled." Wealth, fame, admiration, and all other goals are subordinate and secondary to happiness; whether our desires are material or social, they are merely *means* toward one end: happiness.

Happiness Is…

Just when we believe that we have satisfied a child's curiosity, she will come up with another ploy. From the "infinitely regressive why," she will change course to the "infinitely regressive what" and the "infinitely regressive how." The questions, "What is happiness?" and "How can we attain happiness?" require a more elaborate answer.

Happiness is the emotion that takes into consideration our full and unique nature. I define happiness as "the overall experience of pleasure and meaning." A happy person enjoys positive emotions while perceiving her life as purposeful. The definition does not pertain to a single moment, but to a generalized aggregate of one's experiences: a person can endure emotional pain at times and still be happy overall.

We may think about this definition in terms of the happiness archetype. Pleasure is about the experience of positive emotions in the here and now, about present benefit; meaning comes from having a sense of purpose, from the future benefit of our actions.

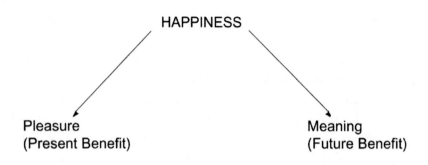

Pleasure

Emotion plays a pivotal role in all our pursuits—including our pursuit of happiness. It is nearly impossible for us to imagine a life devoid of emotion. Think of an emotionless robot that, other than the capacity for emotions, has exactly the same physical and cognitive attributes as humans. The robot thinks and behaves in the same way that humans do. It can discuss deep philosophical issues and follow complex logic; it can dig ditches and build skyscrapers.

As sophisticated as the robot is, however, it lacks all motivation to act. Even the most basic drives are dependent on emotions—the one thing this robot lacks. The robot could not feel the satisfaction of eating or the need to eat; it could not experience the pain associated with hunger or the satisfaction of satiation. The robot would not pursue food and, given that it has the same physical needs of humans, would soon die.

But let us assume that the robot has been programmed to eat and drink regularly. Even then, despite continuing to live on the physical level, the robot would have neither motivation nor incentive to act. Attaining social standing, acquiring wealth, falling in love, would make no difference to it.

Emotions cause *motion*; they provide a *motive* that drives our action. The very language we use suggests an essential truth—that emotion, motion, and motivation are intimately linked. In Latin, *movere* (motion) means "to move," and the prefix "*e*" means "away." The word "motive," source of "motivation," comes from *motivum*, which means "a moving cause." Emotions *move us away* from a desireless state, providing us motivation to act.

The neurologist Antonio Damasio, in writing about a patient, Eliot, who had had a tumor removed from his brain, provides an illuminating real-life example of the link between emotion and motivation. Following surgery, Eliot's cognitive abilities—his memory, arithmetic ability, perceptual ability, and language skills—remained intact. However, the part of Eliot's frontal lobe connected to the ability to experience emotions was damaged in the operation. Eliot's condition was similar to that of the emotionless robot: he had all the physical and cognitive characteristics of a normal human being but the system "involved in feeling and emotion" was damaged.

Eliot's life changed dramatically. Prior to the surgery, he was a happily married, successful lawyer, but after the operation, despite the fact that his "rational brain" was not damaged, Eliot's behavior became so unbearable for those around him, that his wife left him, he lost his job, and he was unable to hold another job for very long. The most striking thing about his predicament was his apathetic reaction: he no longer cared about his relationship or his career.

If we were devoid of emotion and hence of motivation to act, we would aspire to nothing. We would remain indifferent to our actions and thoughts, as well as their ramifications. Because emotion is the foundation of motivation, it naturally plays a central role in our motivation to pursue happiness.

However, merely being capable of emotion—any emotion—is not enough. To be happy, we need the experience of positive emotion; pleasure is a prerequisite for a fulfilling life. According to the psychologist Nathaniel Branden, "Pleasure for man is not a luxury, but a profound psychological need." The total absence of pleasure and the experience of constant emotional pain preclude the possibility of a happy life.

When I write of pleasure, I am not referring to the experience of a constant "high" or ecstasy. We all experience emotional highs and lows; we can experience sadness at times and still lead a happy life. In fact, the unrealistic expectation of a constant high will inevitably lead to disappointment and feelings of inadequacy, and hence to negative emotions. Happiness does not require a constant experience of ecstasy, nor does it require an unbroken chain of positive emotions.[1]

While the happy person experiences highs and lows, his overall state of being is positive. Most of the time he is propelled by positive emotions such as joy and affection rather than negative ones like anger and guilt. Pleasure is the rule; pain, the exception. To be happy, we have to feel that, *on the whole*, whatever sorrows, trials and tribulations we may encounter, we still experience the joy of being alive.

But is living an emotionally gratifying life really enough? Is experiencing positive emotions a *sufficient* condition for happiness? What of a psychotic who experiences euphoric delusions? What of a person who consumes ecstasy-inducing drugs? Are these people happy? The answer is no. Experiencing positive emotions is necessary but not sufficient for happiness.

Meaning

The philosopher Robert Nozick describes a thought experiment that can help us differentiate between the experience of a person on ecstasy-inducing drugs and an experience of true happiness. Nozick asks us to imagine a machine that could provide us with "the experience of writing a great poem or bringing about world peace or loving someone and being loved in return" or any other experience we might desire. The machine could afford us the emotional experience of being in love, which would feel the same as *actually* being in love. We would be unaware that we were plugged

---

1.   In the second meditation I elaborate on the distinction between emotional highs or lows and a deep sense of happiness.

into the machine (that is, we would believe that we were actually spending time with our beloved). Nozick asks whether, given the opportunity, we would *choose* to plug into the machine for the rest of our lives. Another way of asking this question is, would we be happy if we were plugged into the machine for the rest of our lives?

The answer for most of us would clearly be no. We would not want to be hooked up to a machine permanently because we care about "things in addition to how our lives feel to us from the inside." Few of us would think that "only a person's experiences matter." We want not only to take pleasure in experiences, we "want them to be so." There is, then, more to happiness than positive emotions.

Circumventing the cause of these emotions, through a machine or drugs, would be tantamount to *living a lie*. Given the choice between a machine-generated feeling that we had brought about world peace and a less powerful feeling derived from actually helping one person, we would most likely choose the latter. It is as if we have an internal mechanism that demands more than the present sensation that we feel. We need the cause of our emotions to be meaningful. We want to know that our actions have an *actual* effect in the world, not just that we *feel* that they do.

As far as emotions are concerned, human beings are not far removed from animals, and some of the higher animals, chimpanzees, for example, have a similar emotional brain to the one we have. This is not surprising because without emotions (or sensations in the case of animals) there would be no drive to do anything and a living organism would not sustain itself. Without emotions or sensations, animals, like the emotionless robot, would not move.

However, while our capacity for emotions is similar to that of other animals, we are fundamentally different. The fact that we can reflect on the cause of our emotions is one of the characteristics that distinguish us. We have the capacity to reflect on our feelings, thoughts and actions; we have the capacity to be conscious of our consciousness and our experiences.

Another difference between humans and animals is that humans possess the capacity for spirituality. The *Oxford English Dictionary* defines spirituality as "the real sense of significance of something." Animals cannot live a spiritual life; they cannot endow their actions with *meaning* beyond the pleasure or pain that those actions yield.

When speaking of a meaningful life, we often talk of having a sense of purpose, but what we sometimes do not recognize is that finding this sense of purpose entails more than simply setting goals. Goals are necessary if we are to experience a sense of purpose, but having and even reaching our goals does not guarantee that we are leading a purposeful existence. What we need is for the purpose we choose to be intrinsically meaningful.

We could set ourselves the goal of scoring top grades in college or owning a large house, yet still feel empty. To live a meaningful life, the purpose has to be self-generated and must possess *personal significance* rather than being dictated by society's standards and expectations. When we do experience this sense of purpose, we often feel as though we have "found our calling." As George Bernard Shaw said, "This is the true joy in life, the being used for a purpose recognized by yourself as a mighty one."

Different people find meaning in different things. We may find our calling in starting up a business, working in a homeless shelter, raising children, practicing medicine, or making furniture. The important thing is that *we* choose our purpose in accordance with our own values and passions, rather than conforming to others' expectations. To experience happiness, there must be congruency between our choice of action and that which we find meaningful.

Idealism and Realism

I once asked my friend what his calling in life was. He told me that he does not think about his life in terms of calling or some higher purpose: "I am not an idealist," he said, "but a realist."

The realist is considered the pragmatist, the person who has both feet firmly planted on the ground and devotes his time to his day-to-day needs. The idealist is deemed the dreamer, the person who has his eyes toward the horizon and devotes his time to thinking about calling and purpose.

Yet when we set realism and idealism in opposition to one another—when we live as though having ideals and dreams were unrealistic and detached—we are allowing a false dichotomy to hold us back.

Being an idealist *is* being a realist in the deepest sense—it is being true to our *real* nature. We are so constituted that we need our life to have meaning. Without a higher purpose, a calling, an ideal, we cannot attain our full potential for happiness. While I am not advocating dreaming over doing (both are important), there is a significant truth that many realists—rat racers mostly—ignore: *to be idealistic is to be realistic.*

Being an idealist is about having a sense of purpose that encompasses our life as a whole; but to be happy, it is not enough to experience our life as meaningful on the general level of the "big picture." We need to find meaning on the specific level of our daily existence as well. For example, in addition to having the general purpose of creating a happy family or dedicating our life to helping the poor, we also need a specific purpose such as having lunch with our child or spending time at the homeless shelter at night. It is often difficult to sustain ourselves by the thought of a general sense of purpose that lies far off in the horizon: we need a more specific and tangible sense that we are doing something meaningful next week, tomorrow, and later today.

Potential and Happiness

When thinking about the most meaningful life for ourselves, we have to take our potential into consideration. While a cow might seem content with a life spent grazing in the pasture, we cannot be happy living simply to gratify our physical desires. Our inborn potential as humans dictates that we do more, that we utilize our full capacities. "The happiness that is genuinely satisfying," writes the philosopher Bertrand Russell, "is accompanied by the fullest exercise of our faculties and the fullest realization of the world in which we live."

This does not mean that a woman who has the potential to be the most influential person in the world cannot be happy unless she becomes the president of the United States or that a person with the potential to be successful in business cannot be happy unless she makes millions. Becoming the president or a millionaire are *external* manifestations of potential. What I am referring to are *internal* measures of potential. The person with the capacity to be the president could be happy as a scholar of ancient Sanskrit; the person with the capacity to be a millionaire could lead a fulfilling life as a painter. They can find satisfaction if they feel, *from within*, that they are doing things that challenge them, things that use them fully and well.[2]

Success and Happiness

Some people might be concerned that pursuing meaning and pleasure over accolades and wealth could come at the price of success. If, for example, grades and getting into the best institutions no longer constitute a strong motivation, might not a student lose his commitment to his schoolwork? Or, when the next promotion and a pay increase are no longer the ultimate driving force in the workplace, will an employee dedicate less hours to her job?

I had similar concerns about my own success as I was contemplating the shift toward the happiness archetype. The "no pain, no gain" formula had served me well, in terms of quantifiable success, and I feared that my resolve would weaken—that the next milestone would lose its allure and no longer sustain me as it did when I was a rat racer. What happened, however, was the exact opposite.

---

2.   I discuss the importance of challenge in Part II of the book.

The shift from being a rat racer to pursuing happiness is not about working less or with less fervor, but about working as hard or harder at the right activities—those that are a source of both present and future benefit. Similarly, the shift from hedonism to the pursuit of happiness does not entail having less fun; the difference is that the fun the happy person experiences is sustainable, whereas the fun of the hedonist is ephemeral.

There is a synergistic relationship between pleasure and meaning, between present and future benefit. When we derive a sense of purpose from what we do, our experience of pleasure is intensified; and taking pleasure in an activity makes our experience of it all the more meaningful.

The Need for Meaning and Pleasure

Just as pleasure is not sufficient for the attainment of happiness, neither is a sense of purpose. First, it is exceedingly difficult to sustain long-term action, regardless of the meaning we assign to it, without enjoying emotional gratification in the present. The prospect of a brighter future can usually keep us motivated for only a limited time. Second, even if we did sustain our denial of immediate self-gratification, as rat racers often do, we most certainly would not be happy.

In his book, *Man's Search for Meaning*, Viktor Frankl talks about how victims of the Holocaust were able to find meaning in their lives. Despite the physical and emotional torture that these people endured in the concentration camps, some of them found meaning, a sense of purpose, in their meager existence. Their purpose could have been to reunite with loved ones or to some day write about what they had lived through. However, even to suggest that these people were happy while in the camp is absurd. In order to be happy, having meaning in life is not enough. We need the experience of meaning *and* the experience of positive emotions; we need present *and* future benefit.

My theory of happiness draws on the works of Freud and Frankl. Freud's central premise in his psychoanalytic theory is the *pleasure principle*, which says that we are fundamentally driven by the instinctual need for pleasure. Frankl argues that we are motivated by a *will to meaning* rather than by a *will to pleasure*—he says that "striving to find meaning in one's life is the primary motivational force in man." In the context of finding happiness, there is some truth in both Freud's and Frankl's theories. We need to gratify both the will for pleasure and the will for meaning if we are to lead a fulfilling, happy life.[3]

We, especially in the United States, are often criticized for being a society obsessed with happiness: self-help books offering quick-fix solutions and a struggle-free life are selling at an unprecedented rate, and psychiatrists prescribe medication at the first sign of emotional discomfort. While the criticism is, to some extent, justified, it identifies the wrong obsession: the obsession is with pleasure, not with happiness.

The brave new world of quick fixes does not take into consideration long-term benefits and ignores our need for meaning. Happiness presupposes some emotional discomfort and difficult experiences, which some self-help books and psychiatric medication attempt to circumvent.[4] Happiness presupposes our having to overcome obstacles. A struggle-free life is no different from the life in the experience machine, a life that is essentially devoid of meaning. We should remember, too, that going through difficult times augments our capacity for pleasure: it keeps us from taking pleasure for granted, reminds us to be grateful for all the large and small pleasures in our lives. Being grateful in this way can itself be a source of real meaning and pleasure.

---

3.   Another way of characterizing happiness is that it comprises both a cognitive, evaluative component (the meaning we attribute to an experience) and an emotional, affective component (the experience of pleasure).

4.   While I believe that there are cases in which psychiatric medication is warranted and necessary, I am taking issue with the ease with which such medication is dispensed.

Time to be Happy

By recording our daily activities and evaluating them according to how pleasurable and meaningful they are, we can assess our experiences and gain insight into how we can improve the quality of our lives. Devoting a few minutes at the end of each day to write down, and reflect upon, how we spent our time can help us recognize important patterns. For example, we might realize that we spend most of our time in activities that provide future benefit but that we do not enjoy, or doing things that provide us neither meaning nor pleasure. We can then evaluate our lives through the lens of happiness and decide on changes in the form of adding more meaningful and pleasurable experiences.

While there are basic principles that can guide us toward the good life—finding meaning and pleasure, for instance—there is no universal prescription for it. Human beings are complex, multifaceted, and different; each person is unique, a world unto himself. By zooming in on my day to day activities I can see beyond the general principles that govern *a* life and identify the unique needs and wants of *my* life.

We all enjoy different activities, and to varying degrees. For example, writing provides me both present and future benefit, but writing for more than three hours a day bores me. Watching two movies a week contributes to my happiness, whereas four hours a day in front of a screen, over time, will most likely frustrate me. Just because an activity provides us meaning and pleasure does not mean that we can be happy doing it all the time.

To extend the food motif beyond the hamburger, I will introduce what I have come to call the *lasagna principle*—the notion that our capacity to enjoy different activities is limited and unique. Lasagna is my favorite food, and every time I visit my parents, my mother prepares a tray of it that I promptly devour. This does not, however, mean that I want to eat lasagna all day and every day. The same principle applies to my favorite activities, such as writing and watching movies, as well as to my favorite people. Just because my family is the most meaningful thing in my life does not mean that spending eight hours a day with them is what would make me happiest; and not wanting to spend all my waking hours with them does not imply that I love them any less. I derive a great deal of pleasure and meaning from being with my friends, but I also need my daily quota of solitude.

Only the individual, who has access to her inner feelings and thoughts, can identify the activities that provide her with happiness, and the amount of time she would like to spend on each. Identifying the right activity, and then the right quantity for each activity, leads to the highest quality of life.

Happiness Boosters

Change is rarely easy, and habits often persist even if we do recognize the need for a new or altered course of action. A healthy, relatively easy way of bringing about change in the quality of life, is through the gradual introduction of *happiness boosters*—activities, lasting anywhere between a few minutes to a few hours, that provide us both meaning and pleasure, both future and present benefit. For example, we might put aside two evenings each week to engage in our hobby, spend quality time with our family, research a topic of interest, or become involved in political activism.

Introducing happiness boosters into our lives has several advantages. First, it is a more moderate, less risky, approach toward bringing about change. For instance, before making a career move from investment banking to teaching, it is possible to volunteer once a week in an after-school program, in order to be certain that teaching does, indeed, provide us future and present benefit. Alternatively, if we are not happy working in education and want to pursue a career in the money market, we might want to spend some of our free time playing around with stocks to assure ourselves, as much as is possible, that the change we have been imagining will, in fact, make us happier. By affording us the opportunity for trial and error, with minimal risk, happiness boosters can help us hone in on what we want to do most.

A second important benefit of a happiness booster, independent of whether or not we are looking to introduce radical change in our lives, is that it can inspire and invigorate us, acting as both a motivational *pull* and a motivational *push*. For example, the knowledge that, at the end of the day, we are going to spend time with our family—an activity that is both enjoyable and significant for us—can motivate us and pull us through the day, giving us something to look forward to when we get out of bed in the morning. The same happiness booster can then energize us, providing us the push we need by recharging our motivational stores for the next activity.

Ideally, we want our entire day to be filled with happy experiences. This kind of life is not always attainable, though, and it might be that we need to wait until night time or the weekend to pursue activities that provide us present and future benefit. One of the common mistakes that people make is that in their free time, at the end of a hard day at work or in school, they choose to do nothing or vegetate in front of the television screen rather than engage in activities that are both pleasurable and meaningful. In the words of psychologist Mihalyi Csikszentmihalyi, they prefer "mindless hedonism over a mindful challenge." Soon after they engage in their mindless activity, they fall asleep which further reinforces their belief that when they complete their daily chores they are too tired to do anything challenging. In contrast, if instead of doing nothing when we come home from work we turn to our hobbies that challenge us, we are more likely to get our "second wind" and replenish our emotional bank. As the educator Maria Montessori tells us, "To devote oneself to an agreeable task is restful." Happiness boosters, rather than enervating us, lead to ascending levels of energy.

◆   ◆   ◆

The best method of maximizing our levels of happiness is trial and error, paying attention to the quality of our inner experiences. Yet, most of us do not take the time to ask ourselves the question of questions—because we are too busy. As Thoreau says, however, "Life is too short to be in a hurry." If we are always on the go, we are *reacting* to the exigencies of day-to-day life, rather than allowing ourselves the space to *create* a happy life.

The psychologist Abraham Maslow maintains that a person "cannot choose wisely for a life unless he dares to listen to himself, his own self, at each moment in life." It is important to put time aside to take Maslow's dare, to ask ourselves the type of questions that can help us choose wisely: Are the things that I am doing meaningful to me? Is my mind telling me that I should be doing different things with my time? Is my heart telling me that I must change my life? We have to listen, really listen, to our hearts *and* minds—our emotions *and* our reason.

Chapter 3

The Importance of Being Happy

What lies behind us and what lies before us are tiny matters compared to what lies within us.

—*Ralph Waldo Emerson*

Marva Collins is a schoolteacher in Chicago's inner-city, a place where crime and drugs are rampant, and where hope and optimism are scarce. The area's problems are grave and many educators have little faith that their students will be able to escape the destitution and hopelessness that are passed down from one generation to the next.

In 1975, Collins founded the Westside Preparatory School for children in her neighborhood, many of whom had been rejected from other schools for bad behavior or for their inability, for one reason or another, to integrate into the school system. Westside Preparatory was their last chance before the street.

Today, these same children who were once labeled "unteachable" are reading Shakespeare, Emerson, and Euripides by the fourth grade. The children who were once written off as irredeemable failures now go on to college. Collins' students internalize her vision—that each and every student has the potential to succeed; they develop confidence in themselves and are able to imagine and realize a more hopeful future.

Marva Collins founded her school with very little money, initially using her house as a classroom. For the next twenty years she continued to struggle financially and was often on the verge of closure. Today, there are Marva Collins schools in several states; educators from all over the world come to Chicago to meet with her, learn her methods, and be inspired by her.

Collins' experience provides an insight into the implications of recognizing happiness as the ultimate end. She says that when "in the company of people who run multibillion [dollar] corporations and who have amassed fortunes," she asks herself time and again why she wants to be a teacher. Collins finds an answer as she reflects on one of her students, Tiffany,

> a child considered autistic and who had not spoken, who had been told by the experts that she was an unlovable and unteachable child. Then one day after much patience, prayers, love, and determination, Tiffany's first words to me were "I love you Mrs. Ollins." The consonant "C" was left off; but I realized that the tears that flowed from Tiffany's declaration made me the wealthiest woman in the world. Today, to see Tiffany writing her numerals, beginning to read single words, talking, and most of all to see that glee in her eyes that says, I too, am special, I too, can learn—this to me is worth all of the gold in Fort Knox.

Of another student whose life was transformed by Westside Preparatory School, Collins writes, "It is worth all the sleepless nights wondering how I am going to balance our deficits to see the glow in [his] eyes that will one day light the world."

Marva Collins could have made a fortune. She could have avoided worrying about closures and deficits. In the 1980s, she could have accepted the Reagan and Bush administrations' offers of the post of secretary of education and all the honor and prestige that that would bring her, but

Marva Collins loves to teach and believes that she can make the most significant difference in the classroom.

Teaching gives her life meaning that she believes no other profession could give her; teaching gives her the emotional gratification that no amount of money could buy. She feels that she is "the wealthiest woman in the world" and that her experiences as a teacher are worth more to her than "all of the gold in Fort Knox" because *happiness, not gold or prestige, is the ultimate currency.*

Happiness as the Ultimate Currency

If we wanted to assess the worth of a business, we would use money as our means of measurement. We would calculate the dollar value of its assets and liabilities, profits and losses. Anything that could not be translated into monetary terms would not increase or decrease the business' value. In this case—in measuring a company's worth—money is the ultimate currency.

A human being, like a business, makes profits and suffers losses. For a human being, however, the ultimate currency is not money, nor is it any external measure such as fame, fortune, or power. The ultimate currency for a human being is happiness.

Money and fame are subordinate to happiness and have no *intrinsic* value. The only reason money and fame may be desirable is that having them, or the thought of having them, could lead to positive emotions or meaning. In themselves, wealth and fame are worthless: there would be no reason to seek fame and fortune if they did not contribute, in some way, toward happiness. In the same sense that owned goods are secondary to money in a business—in that their worth is evaluated in dollars and cents—fame and material wealth are secondary to happiness in our lives.

The ramifications of understanding that happiness is the ultimate currency are dramatic. To take an extreme example, if we were offered the choice between a million dollars and a conversation with a friend, we should choose the one that would give us more overall happiness. If the conversation provided more emotional gratification and meaning than a million dollars, then we should choose the conversation. Using the ultimate currency as the standard, we would profit more if we were to choose the conversation.

Weighing the value of a conversation against money may seem like comparing apples to oranges. But by translating money, conversations, or anything else for that matter into the currency of happiness, through evaluating how happy something makes us, we have a common currency that enables us to compare seemingly unrelated experiences.

Needless to say, the choice between a million dollars and a conversation is not so simple. In order to choose wisely, it is insufficient to say that we enjoy speaking to our friend more and should therefore forgo the million dollars. A large sum of money can provide security in the future, and that may prevent certain negative emotions in the long run. In addition, a million dollars can provide the freedom and opportunity to take on meaningful tasks. If, however, after taking the full context into consideration, we find that the conversation will yield more pleasure and meaning, then it is ultimately of more value to us than a million dollars. As the psychologist Carl Jung said, "The least of things with a meaning is worth more in life than the greatest of things without it."

Imagine the following scenario. An alien from Venus walks into a shop and asks to purchase an item worth one thousand dollars. She offers the shop owner the choice between a thousand dollars or a bill that, on Venus, is equivalent to a million Earth dollars. The shop owner knows that he will never get to Venus and that Venusian money has no value on Earth. Unless he wants to keep the money for its sentimental value, the shop owner should choose the thousand Earth dollars. Venusian currency is only as valuable as the sum it can yield in the currency that is accepted on Earth.

Likewise, a million dollars is only as valuable as the sum it can yield in the ultimate currency. Just as Earth money is the ultimate currency in which a business is paid, and hence the currency that matters, happiness is the ultimate currency in which a human being is paid, and thus the currency that matters. Happiness should be the determinant of our actions, the goal toward which all other goals lead.

Wealth and Happiness

Money—beyond the bare minimum necessary for food and shelter (and I am not talking caviar and castles)—is nothing more than a means to an end. Yet so often we confuse means with ends, and sacrifice happiness (end) for money (means).

It is easy to do this when material wealth is elevated to the position of the ultimate end, as it so often is in our society. This is not to say that the accumulation and production of material wealth is in itself wrong. Material prosperity can help individuals, as well as society, attain higher levels of happiness. Financial security can liberate us from work we do not find meaningful and from having to worry about the next paycheck. Moreover, the desire to make money can challenge and inspire us. Even so, it is not the money per se that is valuable, but the fact that it can potentially yield more positive experiences. Material wealth in and of itself does not necessarily generate meaning or lead to emotional wealth.

Studies have shown that the relationship between wealth and happiness is very different from what most of us would expect. In extensive cross-cultural and longitudinal studies of happiness, psychologist Ed Diener and his colleagues found a very low correlation between material wealth and happiness, except in cases of extreme poverty where people's basic needs were not being met. Moreover, although for the last fifty years each generation of Americans has become wealthier, studies reveal no change in levels of happiness.

Surprisingly, some people feel more depressed once they have attained material prosperity than they did while striving for it. The rat racer is sustained by the hope that his actions will yield some future benefit, which makes his negative emotions more bearable. However, once he reaches his destination, and realizes that material prosperity does not make him happy, there is nothing to sustain him. He is filled with a sense of despair and hopelessness, because there is nothing else to look forward to, nothing that would allow him to envision a future in which he would be happy.

So if material wealth does not inevitably lead to happiness, why the obsession with it? Why does being rich take precedence over finding meaning? Why do we feel so much more comfortable making decisions based on materialistic criteria than emotional ones?

Taking an evolutionary approach, it could be that our distant past determines our current behavior. When we were still hunters and gatherers, the accumulation of wealth—of food, primarily—would often determine whether we would survive the next drought or the next cold winter. Hoarding became part of our constitution. Today, even those of us whose futures are materially secure still have the tendency to hoard far beyond our needs. The accumulation of wealth is no longer a means toward survival, but an end in itself. We no longer accumulate to live; we live to accumulate.

In making decisions and judgments, we also tend to focus on the material rather than paying heed to the emotional because those things that are quantifiable lend themselves more easily to assessment and evaluation. We value the measurable, material wealth and prestige, over the unmeasurable, emotions and meaning. As Laurence G. Boldt says in *Zen and the Art of Making a Living*, "society tells us the only thing that matters is matter—the only things that count are the things that can be counted." The monetary worth of a house is quantifiable; the feelings we attach to our home are not. Shakespeare's *Hamlet* may cost ten dollars in the bookstore; what it means to us cannot be measured.

Emotional Bankruptcy

While we are accumulating material wealth, we are nearing bankruptcy in the currency that truly matters. Just as a business can go bankrupt, so can a human being. To remain solvent, a business needs to make profits; that is, its income has to exceed its expenses.

In thinking about our lives, it may be helpful to think of positive experiences as income and negative ones as expenses. When our positive experiences outweigh our negative ones, we have made a profit in the ultimate currency. Long-term depression may be seen as a sort of emotional bankruptcy—the duration and intensity of negative experiences (losses) overwhelm the positive ones (income).

An entire society can face the prospect of bankruptcy—a great depression—if the percentage of individual bankruptcies rises continuously. Today, as the rates of anxiety and depression rise, society heads toward emotional bankruptcy in the ultimate currency. So while we are making huge strides forward in science and technology—in our material welfare—we are rapidly falling further and further back in terms of our emotional predicament.

Unfortunately, there are no signs that things are improving. Approximately one-third of American teenagers suffer from depression. Studies in the United States, Europe, Australia, and Asia indicate that children today experience more anxiety and depression than children did in previous generations. This trend extends across ethnic and socio-economic lines.

In his book *Emotional Intelligence*, Daniel Goleman notes that "Each successive generation worldwide since the opening of the century has lived with a higher risk than their parents of suffering a major depression—not just sadness, but a paralyzing listlessness, dejection, and self-pity, and an overwhelming hopelessness—over the course of life." What Goleman is pointing to here is the increase, society-wide, in the prevalence of emotional bankruptcy. The "overwhelming hopelessness"—the resignation—that Goleman describes results from our sense that we are unable to overcome this impoverished emotional state, on either the individual or the global level.

According to Goleman, the "Age of Anxiety" that characterized the twentieth century is now evolving into an "Age of Melancholy." In *Man's Search for Meaning*, Viktor Frankl claims that the "existential vacuum is a widespread phenomenon of the twentieth century" and laments the fact that 25 percent of his European students and 60 percent of his American students feel that they live in an "existential vacuum," a state of "inner emptiness, a void within themselves."

The situation today is worse than it was in 1950 when Frankl wrote his book, and a more recent survey (*New York Times*, January 12, 1998) of students entering American colleges may help to explain why. In 1968, college freshmen were asked what their personal goals were: 41 percent wanted to make a lot of money and 83 percent wanted to develop a meaningful philosophy of life. The pattern was significantly different in 1997, when 75 percent of freshmen said their goal was to be very well off financially and 41 percent wanted to develop a meaningful philosophy of life. As larger numbers of people come to perceive material wealth as an end in itself, and, thus, as more individual members of society are unhappy, society as a whole nears a state of emotional bankruptcy.

With emotional bankruptcy come some of our most disturbing social problems—including drug and alcohol abuse and religious fanaticism. It is easy to see why an unhappy person might take drugs if they provide him a temporary escape from the reality of his joyless life, or why someone might turn to religious fanaticism if a charismatic preacher proffers the possibility of eternal happiness.

◆   ◆   ◆

So what can we do to reverse the trend toward emotional bankruptcy? The next part of this book is dedicated to the application of the theory of happiness: I explore the ways in which we can enhance meaning and pleasure in schools, in the workplace, and in relationships.

PART II

Happiness Applied
In School, at Work, and
with Our Loved Ones

Chapter 4

Happiness and Education

Upon [the educator] devolves the responsibility for instituting the conditions for the kind of present experiences which have a favorable effect upon the future.

—*John Dewey*

My brother studies psychology at Harvard. Before he came to school, he spent his free time reading psychology, discussing it, writing and thinking about it. Now, however, he says he dislikes it.

His feeling is not unique: most students dislike school work. What, then, motivates them to devote so much time to their studies? While talking to my brother about his unhappiness at school, I came up with two models that illustrate how students are motivated: the drowning model and the lovemaking model.

The drowning model shows two things: that the desire to free ourselves of pain can be a strong motivator, and that, once freed, we can easily mistake our relief for happiness. A person whose head is forced under water will suffer discomfort and pain and will struggle to escape. If, at the last moment, his head is released, he will gasp for air and experience a sense of intoxicating relief.

The situation may be less dramatic for students who do not enjoy school, but the nature of their motivation—the need to avoid a negative consequence—is similar. Throughout the term, drowning in work that they do not enjoy, students are motivated by their fear of failure. At the end of the term, liberated from their books and papers and exams, they feel an overwhelming sense of relief—which, in the moment, can feel a lot like happiness.

This pattern of pain followed by relief is the model that is imprinted upon us from grade school. It is easy to see how, unaware of alternative models, living as a rat racer could seem like the most normal and attractive prospect.

The lovemaking model, however, offers a different way of thinking about learning, one that can encompass both present and future benefit. The many wonderful hours that we put into reading, researching, thinking, and writing can be looked upon as foreplay. The Eureka experience—when the boundary between knowledge and intuition breaks, when we reach a solution to a problem, for instance—is like the orgasm. As in the drowning model, there is a desirable end goal, but in the lovemaking model, we derive satisfaction from everything we do along the way.

Ensuring that the process of learning is itself enjoyable is, in part, the responsibility of each student, especially in college and graduate school, when they have more independence. Yet by the time students are mature enough to take responsibility for their education, most have already internalized the rat racer's ethos. They learn from their parents that grades and titles are the measure of success, that their responsibility is to produce outstanding report cards rather than to enjoy learning for learning's sake. Educators—parents and teachers—who care about helping children lead happy lives must first themselves believe that happiness is the ultimate currency. Children are extremely sensitive to cues, and will internalize their educators' beliefs even when these beliefs are implicit.

In school, children should be encouraged to pursue the paths that afford them pleasure and meaning. If a student wants to be a social worker, and has taken the time to consider the costs and benefits thereof, then his teachers should encourage him despite the fact that being a lawyer might yield more money; if he wants to become a businessman, then his parents should support him, even though their wish had always been that he pursue medicine. For parents and teachers who believe that happiness is the ultimate currency, this is the natural and logical thing to do.[1]

In emphasizing achievements (which are tangible) over the cultivation of a love of learning (which is intangible), schools simultaneously reinforce the rat-race mentality and stifle children's emotional development. The rat racer learns that emotional gratification is secondary to the kind of achievements that others can recognize and validate, that emotions only get in the way of success, and are best ignored or suppressed.

The irony is that emotions are not only necessary for the pursuit of the ultimate currency, but for the attainment of material success as well. Daniel Goleman, in *Emotional Intelligence*, says, "Psychologists agree that IQ contributes only about 20 percent of the factors that determine success. A full 80 percent comes from other factors, including what I call emotional intelligence." The mindset of the rat racer is antithetical to emotional intelligence and thus to a happy *and* successful life.

What, then, can teachers and parents do to help students experience pleasure in school, and at the same time perform well? How can achievement and the love of learning be reconciled? The work of psychologist Mihalyi Csikszentmihalyi on "flow" provides us with important insights and guidelines on how we can create a home and school environment that is conducive to the experience of present and future benefit, pleasure and meaning.

---

1. I am not advocating a *laissez faire* approach to education in which parents simply cater to their children's whims, allowing them to indulge their immediate likes or dislikes. The most successful educators find a balance between externally imposed boundaries and democratic practices, between firmness and allowing for independence. For a more in-depth discussion of child rearing and educational practices see Lillard's *Montessori Today* and Ginott's *Teacher and Child: A Book for Parents and*

Flow

Flow, according to Csikszentmihalyi, is "a dynamic state that characterizes consciousness when experience is attended to for its own sake." It describes a state in which one is immersed in an experience that is rewarding in and of itself, a state in which we feel we are one with the experience, in which "action and awareness are merged."[2]

We all know what it feels like to be so absorbed in reading a book or writing a paper that we fail to hear our name being called. Or, while cooking a meal or talking to a friend or playing basketball in the neighborhood park, we discover that hours have gone by when it seemed that only minutes had passed. These are flow experiences.

When in a state of flow we enjoy both peak experience *and* peak performance: we experience pleasure and perform at our best. Athletes often refer to this experience as being in "the zone." Whatever we do in a state of flow—whether kicking a ball, carving wood, writing a poem, or studying for an exam—we are completely focused on our activity; nothing distracts us or competes for our attention. Performing at our best, we learn, grow, improve, and advance toward our future purpose.

Csikszentmihalyi explains that having goals, having a clear sense of purpose, is necessary in order to attain flow. While goals can and do change over time, the direction of the activity has to be unambiguous while we are performing it. When we are not distracted by all the other possible things we could be doing, when we are wholeheartedly committed to our objective, we are free to devote ourselves fully to the task at hand. In flow, present and future benefit merge: a clear future goal is not in opposition, but rather contributes, to the experience of the here and now. Flow experiences lead to higher levels of happiness by transforming the formula of "no pain, no gain" to "present gain, future gain."

---

2. Csikszentmihalyi's work on flow has wide implications for the individual and for society. For a more complete discussion see *Finding Flow*.

Csikszentmihalyi's studies of flow show that the "no pain, no gain" model is based on the myth that only through extreme and sustained overexertion can we attain our optimal level of performance. Research on flow shows that pain is not, in fact, the optimal condition for peak performance. Rather, there is specific zone where we not only perform at our best but also enjoy what we are doing. We reach this zone when our activities provide the appropriate level of challenge, when the task at hand is neither too difficult nor too easy.

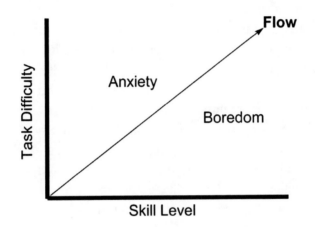

The graph shows that if the difficulty of a task is high and our skill level low, then we experience anxiety; if our skill levels are high and the difficulty of the task is low, we experience boredom. We experience flow when the difficulty of the task and our skill level correspond.

Because many students experience either boredom or anxiety in school, they neither enjoy it nor perform at their best. For students to derive more present and future benefit from school, teachers should, whenever possible, structure lessons and activities to meet each individual student's skill level.

The Privilege of Challenge

A task that is appropriately difficult may involve struggle on the child's part. Educators, especially parents, confusing struggle with hardship—and wanting to protect their children from hardship—commonly make the mistake of catering to their children's every wish and rescuing them from every challenge. In trying to provide a "privileged" life for their children, these parents deny them the opportunity to struggle, which keeps them from experiencing the satisfaction of overcoming challenges—and deprives them of the ultimate currency.

Samuel Smiles, the father of the modern self-help movement, wrote in 1858 that "Every youth should be made to feel that his happiness and well-doing in life must necessarily rely mainly on himself and the exercise of his own energies, rather than upon the help and patronage of others." Parents who "help" their children circumvent hard work can lead to much unhappiness in the long run: "It is doubtful whether any heavier curse could be imposed on man than the complete gratification of all his wishes without effort on his part, leaving nothing for his hopes, desires or struggles." When challenged, children, like adults, will find meaning in their accomplishments and enjoy the process of attaining their goals.

◆   ◆   ◆

Rather than helping students find meaningful and challenging goals and activities, rather than helping students experience the joy of learning, many educators are more concerned with getting students to score well on exams. Csikszentmihalyi writes:

> Neither parents nor schools are very effective at teaching the young to find pleasure in the right things. Adults, themselves often deluded by infatuation with fatuous models, conspire in the deception. They make serious tasks seem dull and hard,

and frivolous ones exciting and easy. Schools generally fail to teach how exciting, how mesmerizingly beautiful science or mathematics can be; they teach the routine of literature or history rather than the adventure.

The love of learning is hardwired: young children are always asking questions, are always eager to find out more about the world around them. Educators who support children in the pursuit of the things that are important to them, and who help children attain flow experiences, cultivate this innate love of learning. They can turn education into a mesmerizingly beautiful adventure—the life-long pursuit of the ultimate currency.

Chapter 5

Happiness in the Workplace

○ ○

Taste the joy that springs from labor.

—*Henry Wadsworth Longfellow*

Five years ago I met a young man, a corporate lawyer, who was working in a prestigious New York firm and was about to be made a partner. He owned a luxury apartment overlooking Central Park and had just bought a new BMW, for cash.

He worked extremely hard, spending at least sixty hours each week in the office. Every morning he had to drag himself out of bed to get there, for he felt that he had very little to which he could look forward—the meetings with clients and colleagues, the legal briefs and contracts that filled his days, were nothing more to him than a series of chores to be gotten through.

When I asked him what he would do for a living in an ideal world, he said that he would work in an art gallery. Were no jobs available in art galleries? No, no, he said, there were jobs. Was he not qualified to find work? He was. But working in an art gallery, he said, would entail a steep loss of income and lowered standard of living. He hated the law firm but saw no way out.

Here was a man who was unhappy because he felt enslaved to a job he disliked. Yet my conversation with him made clear to me that he was enslaved not because he had no choice, but because he had made a choice that made him unhappy—prioritizing material wealth over pleasure and meaning.

Slave to Passions

In Hebrew, the word for "work"—*avoda*—stems from the same root as the word for "slave"—*eved*. Most of us have no choice but to work for a living. Even if we do not need to work for our survival, we are enslaved by our nature: we are constituted to want to be happy, and to be happy we need to work.

However, being enslaved by the exigencies of life and by our constitution does not preclude the possibility that we can *feel* free. We experience freedom when we *choose* a path that provides us both meaning and pleasure. Whether our subjective experience of work is of freedom or not depends on whether we choose to be slaves to material wealth or to emotional prosperity, slaves to others' expectations or to our passions.

To make such choices, we might begin by asking some questions of ourselves. Ask and you shall receive, say the Scriptures. When we ask questions we open ourselves up to new quests and conquests: we see things we may not have seen before, discover paths that were previously obscured.

By posing a series of genuine questions, we challenge our assumptions, our conventional ways of thinking about what is possible in our lives: Am I happy at work? How can I become happier? Can I leave my job and find something meaningful and pleasurable? If I cannot afford to leave, what can I do to make my work more enjoyable?

The right employer can create conditions that are conducive to happiness. We cannot, though, simply hope that the right job will be handed to us; we have to actively seek and create meaning and pleasure in the workplace. Blaming others—our parents, our teachers, our boss, or the government—may yield sympathy, but not happiness. The ultimate responsibility for finding the right job or creating the right conditions at work lies with us.

In some jobs it is possible to restructure work to meet the conditions necessary for the attainment of the ultimate currency. For example, we can experience flow by setting clear goals and challenging ourselves even when our job does not require that we do so. We can assume more responsibility and seek higher levels of involvement in work that we find interesting; we can take initiative and look for areas where we can contribute more to the organization. If, however, the setup of our job is such that it is impossible for us to feel interested and engaged, no matter how hard we try, then we might choose to look for an alternative source of income. While in some cases leaving our current workplace might not seem to be a feasible option, in most cases we can find an alternative—a workplace that, beyond the hard currency necessary for our basic material needs, will provide us with the ultimate currency.

Committing to change within the workplace or looking for a new job can be frightening. However, change is necessary if we are stuck in a job that, beyond our material needs, supplies us with little else. Had we found ourselves in a job that did not afford us our basic material needs, we would do everything in our power to change our predicament. So why do we set lower standards for ourselves when the ultimate currency—when our own happiness—is at stake? What we need if we are to implement change in our lives is courage. And *courage is not about not having fear, but about having fear and going ahead anyway.*

Hard currency and the ultimate currency are both necessary for our survival, and they are *not* mutually exclusive. Moreover, because we often perform best at the things that we find most engaging, pursuing those activities that provide us meaning and pleasure could actually lead to more quantifiable success in the long run. We naturally work harder at the things that we care about and are interested in—that we are passionate about. Without passion, motivation wanes; with passion, motivation increases, and, over time, so does ability.

The investment we make in our work cannot be determined merely by what we stand to gain or lose financially. Without having an emotional investment in our work, we ultimately lose interest. Emotions lead to motion—they are our fuel.

Finding the Ultimate Job

The psychologist Abraham Maslow once wrote that "the most beautiful fate, the most wonderful good fortune that can happen to any human being, is to be paid for doing that which he passionately loves to do."

It is not always easy to discover what sort of work might yield this "good fortune" in the ultimate currency. It takes a conscious and concerted effort to find the work that really suits us, because we are usually encouraged to pursue what we do well rather than what we want to do. Most career advisors and job placement tests focus us on our strengths rather than on our passions. Questions such as "What am I good at?" are of course important in selecting work, but we must ask them only after we have identified what gives us meaning and pleasure. When our first question is "What *can* I do?" we give priority to quantifiable currencies (money and the approval of others); when our first question is "What do I *want* to do?"—what gives me meaning and pleasure?—our choice is driven by our pursuit of the ultimate currency.

The Three Question Process (TQP)

Finding the right job—a job that corresponds to both our passions and our strengths—is often challenging. We can begin the process by asking these three crucial questions—What gives me *meaning*? What gives me *pleasure*? What are my *strengths*?—and noting the trends that emerge. Looking at the answers, identifying areas of overlap, can help us determine what kind of work would make us happiest.[1]

Generating accurate answers to these questions requires more effort than simply jotting down whatever leaps to mind when, for instance, we try to think about what gives us meaning. Most of us have more or less ready-made answers to such questions; these answers are usually true, but

---

1.   For a more elaborate discussion of identifying personal strengths see Buckingham and Clifton's *Now, Discover Your Strengths.*

may stop short of representing the full range of experiences that we have found meaningful. We may need to spend time reflecting, thinking deeply to recall those moments in our lives when we felt a sense of true purpose.

We may also need to spend some time considering the answers to the three questions: the lists we generate may be long and the way in which we phrase our answers may not make the areas of overlap immediately apparent.

Using the TQP

Our lists will probably be messier and less straightforward than the following example, which is meant to show how the process works in its most basic form—how thinking about meaning, pleasure, and our strengths can lead us to more happiness and success.

Say I derive meaning from solving problems, working with children, engaging in political activism, and music. I enjoy sailing, cooking, music, and being around children. My strengths are my sense of humor, my enthusiasm, my ability to relate to children, and my problem-solving skills.

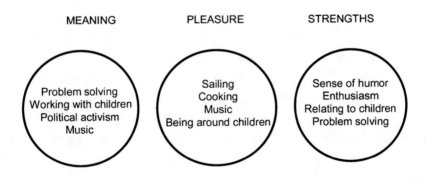

MEANING	PLEASURE	STRENGTHS
Problem solving Working with children Political activism Music	Sailing Cooking Music Being around children	Sense of humor Enthusiasm Relating to children Problem solving

Which of the answers overlap?

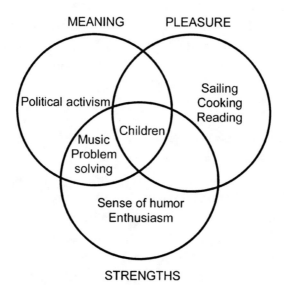

In looking at the diagram, I can clearly determine that I should work with children. To figure out what specific jobs would be best for me, I would now take into consideration some other aspects of my personality and my life. For example, I am highly organized and like to plan my week's work in advance—therefore, I prefer to have a more structured daily schedule. I like to travel and it would therefore be important for me to have a job that allows long breaks.

So what kind of work with children would provide a structured daily schedule and long breaks? What kind of work might involve or make the best use of my other passions and skills, such as my enthusiasm, my sense of humor, my love of reading and problem solving? Taking all of these factors into consideration I might consider becoming an English teacher. While the process may not have led me to the most financially remunerative job, it may have helped me to identify the work that is most profitable to me in the ultimate currency.[2]

The TQP can function as a useful tool for the manager. Helping her employees identify and perform activities that they enjoy, find meaningful, and are good at, will yield more commitment and better overall performance. The TQP might even be more useful for a manager selecting new employees. Not every workplace can satisfy the needs, and tap the strengths, of every person. It is important for the manager to create, from the outset, a fit between those she hires and what the workplace has to offer.

Prejudice Against Work

Adam and Eve lived the quintessential life of leisure—they did not work and did not plan for the future. Yet when they ate the forbidden fruit, they were banished from the Garden of Eden and they and their descendants were condemned to lives of hard work.

The notion of hard work as punishment has become so embedded in our culture that we tend to depict heaven—the ideal place in which we would have the ideal life—as devoid of every hardship, including work. As it turns out, though, here on earth we do need to work to be happy.

In their study of "Optimal Experience In Work and Leisure," Csikszentmihalyi and Lefevre show that people prefer leisure to work, a conclusion that no one would find startling. However, they also discovered something else: that people actually have more flow experiences at work than they do at home.

This paradox—that we say we prefer leisure at the same time that we are having our peak experiences at work—is strange and revealing. It suggests

---

2.   The TQP can also help us make important decisions in other areas of our lives. When choosing a class in school, for example, we can look for an overlap between courses that would be meaningful for our future career, that we would enjoy, and that we would be good at.

that our prejudice against work, our association of effort with pain and leisure with pleasure, is so deep-rooted that it distorts our perception of the actual experience. When we automatically and regularly evaluate positive experiences at work negatively, simply as a learned response, we are severely limiting our potential for happiness—because in order to be happy we must not only experience positive emotions, but also evaluate them as such.

When our vision of happiness is rigid—when it precludes the possibility that effort and struggle can be sources of the ultimate currency—we overlook some of the best prospects we have to create a fulfilling life. At work, we fail to recognize and realize opportunities for happiness; outside of work, we squander our "free" time by freeing it of effort, challenge, and, hence, of much meaning. We are then left with a feeling that happiness is hopelessly elusive.

◆   ◆   ◆

In *Zen and the Art of Motorcycle Maintenance*, Pirsig writes, "The truth knocks on the door and you say, 'Go away, I'm looking for the truth' and so it goes away." When we view work as punishment and leisure as a chance to do nothing, we fail to recognize the rich sources of pleasure and meaning that are right in front of us. But when we understand the true nature of the ultimate currency, work, like play, can become pleasurable and yield present benefit; play, like work, can become meaningful and provide future benefit.

Chapter 6

Happiness and Love

o o o o o o o o o o o o o o o o o o o o o o o o o o o o o o o o o o o o o o

All who could win joy must share it; happiness was born a twin.

—Byron

To be Loved for Who We Are

One afternoon, a few weeks after winning the Israeli squash championship, I turned to my mother, and, with the earnestness that only a self-important sixteen-year-old can muster, said: "I want women to want me for who I am, not for being the national champion." I am not entirely sure how much I was expressing a true concern (given the scarcity in Israel of squash courts, players, and, alas, fans), and how much I was driven by false modesty—imitating the rich and famous who complain how hard it is to find someone to love them for who they "really" are. In truth, I was not much worried about being wanted for who I was; I simply wanted to be wanted.

Whatever my actual motivation for raising this issue might have been, my mother responded to it as seriously as she did to all the other grave concerns I seemed to have in those days. She said, "Your being the national champion *is* a reflection of who you are, of, among other things, your passion and dedication." As my mother understood the situation, winning the championship merely made certain qualities more visible. The external attracted more attention to the internal.

It took me a few years to grasp how what my mother meant by being loved for who we are differed from my own nebulous understanding of this concept. What does it mean to be wanted or loved for "who we really are"? To put it another way, what are we talking about when we talk about "unconditional love," a phrase we throw around in the bedroom, the children's room, the classroom? Do we mean that we want someone to love us for no reason? To love us no matter what? Are we saying that love needs no justification?

Talking about love simply as a feeling, as an emotion or state independent of reason, is reductive. Love cannot last without a rational foundation: just as positive emotions are insufficient for lasting happiness (the hedonist cannot sustain happiness because there is no meaning in his life), so strong feelings, in and of themselves, are insufficient to sustain love. When a man falls in love with a woman he does so for certain conscious or unconscious *reasons*. He may *feel* that he just loves her "for who she is," but not be sure what he means by that; when asked to articulate why he loves her he might respond, "I don't know, I just do." We are taught that falling in love with someone is about following our heart, not our mind— that love, by definition, is inexplicable, mystical, beyond reason. However, if it really is love that he feels, he does feel it for a reason. These reasons might not be conscious and accessible, but they nevertheless exist.

If, then, there are actual reasons for loving someone, if there are certain *conditions* under which we fall in love, can there be such a thing as unconditional love? Or, is the idea of unconditional love fundamentally unreasonable? It depends on whether or not the characteristics we love in someone are manifestations of that person's core self.

The Core Self

The core self encompasses our deepest and most stable characteristics— our character. It comprises the actual principles by which we live, which are not necessarily synonymous with the ones we claim to follow. Because we cannot observe a core self directly, the only way for us to know a person's character is through its manifestations, through the person's behavior, which *is* observable.

A person who is empathetic, assiduous, patient, and enthusiastic—whose core self comprises these characteristics—might establish an intervention program for underprivileged children. The success or failure of the program, which is contingent on any number of external factors, may have nothing to do with "who she is"; it is the internal characteristics that led her to start the program that are part of her core self. Her behavior (starting the program) reflects her core self, whereas the outcome of her behavior (whether or not the program succeeds) does not. If someone loved her unconditionally he would of course be delighted by the program's success and saddened by its failure; either way, though, his feelings toward *her* would not change because her core self would not have changed.

To be loved for our wealth, power, or fame is to be loved conditionally; to be loved for our steadfastness, intensity, or warmth is to be loved unconditionally.

The Circle of Happiness

The psychologist Donald W. Winnicott observed that children playing in close proximity to their mothers display higher levels of creativity in their games than those who are farther away. Children are highly creative as long as they are within a certain radius of their mothers, within a *circle of creativity* of sorts. The circle of creativity is a space in which children can take risks and try things out, fall and stand up again, fail and succeed—because they feel secure and safe in the presence of a person who loves them unconditionally.

Because we, as adults, are capable of higher levels of abstraction than children, we do not always have to be physically near our loved ones to be within their circle of creativity. The knowledge that we are loved unconditionally creates a psychological space of safety and security.

Unconditional love creates a parallel *circle of happiness*—a space in which we are encouraged to pursue those things that are meaningful and pleasurable for us. We experience the freedom to follow our passions—whether in art, banking, teaching, or gardening—regardless of prestige or success. Unconditional love is the foundation of a happy relationship.

If someone truly loves me, he or she, *more than anything else*, would want me to express my core self and would draw out those qualities that make me who I really am.

Meaning and Pleasure in Love

While unconditional love is necessary for a happy relationship, it is, in and of itself, insufficient. Just as meaning and pleasure, future and present benefit, are essential for sustained happiness at work and at school, so are they essential for a happy relationship.

Couples who get together primarily for some future gain—because being together will help them get ahead in some way, socially or financially, for example—are in rat-race relationships. So are those couples who justify working hard and spending little time with each other on the grounds that they are doing so for the sake of the relationship—to ensure a secure and happy future together. While it is sometimes necessary to forgo present benefit for the sake of future goals, spending too much time living for the future will ultimately lead to the relationship's failure.

At the other extreme we have the hedonist, who enters into and evaluates a relationship primarily on the basis of how much pleasure it provides. Mistaking pleasure for happiness, the hedonist in a relationship mistakes lust for love. The hedonist's pleasure inevitably fades, though, because without a meaningful foundation to the relationship that goes beyond immediate gratification, it is impossible to sustain happiness.

A relationship that is based on either future benefit or present benefit will ultimately lead to unhappiness. Unhappy partners who choose to remain together have usually resigned themselves to the notion that happiness is unattainable in a long-term relationship.

Love and Sacrifice

Yet even people who believe that happiness might be attainable with the right person may resign themselves to unhappy relationships out of a sense of duty toward their partners, their children, or the institution of marriage. They believe, mistakenly, that sacrifice is synonymous with virtue, failing to recognize that staying in the relationship for the "sake" of the other will lead them both to frustration and unhappiness. Over time, the person sacrificing will resent his partner for depriving him of the meaning or pleasure he might find elsewhere. His partner, in turn, will be miserable knowing that he remains with her because he *has* to, not because he *wants* to, and thus, she too will lose any meaning or pleasure she might have derived from the relationship.

Even within a relationship in which partners love each other and want to be together, happiness can be undermined by the belief that sacrifice is synonymous with love—that the greater the sacrifice, the deeper the love.

It is important to note that standing by one's partner in a time of need is not sacrifice; when we love someone we often feel that helping that person is helping ourselves. When I speak of sacrifice here, I am speaking of a person renouncing something that is essential to his or her happiness. For example, a woman permanently giving up a job she loves and cannot find elsewhere so that her husband can take a job abroad *is* sacrificing— because if her work is fundamental to her core self, abandoning it is detrimental to her happiness. The same woman taking a week off from work because she wants to help her husband with an important project is not necessarily sacrificing—she may not be compromising her core self in any way, and thus may not be compromising her happiness. Moreover, because her happiness is intertwined with his, because each of them is happier when the other is happy, helping him is also helping herself.

There is no easy way to distinguish between behavior that is sacrificial, and hence destructive to the long-term success of the relationship, and behavior that is conducive to the growth of the relationship. The only way to begin to sort out the harmful from the beneficial is by evaluating the relationship, as a whole, in the currency of happiness.

A relationship is a transaction in the ultimate currency. Like every transaction, the more profitable a relationship is for *both* people, the more likely it is to flourish. When one of the partners is shortchanged in the ultimate currency—when she is constantly giving up meaning and pleasure so that he can have more of it—both partners end up less happy in the long run. In order to feel satisfied within a relationship we have to feel that the transaction is equitable.

Psychologist Elaine Hatfield, who studies relationships, shows that people do not like being "overpaid" or "underpaid" in a relationship; both partners feel more content, and the relationship as a whole is more likely to prosper, when the relationship is perceived as equitable by both. This does not mean that both partners should bring home the same paycheck; the unit of evaluation used in this kind of transaction is not dollars and cents, but the ultimate currency. While compromise is, of course, a natural part of any relationship, while at different times each partner will forgo some meaning or pleasure for the sake of the other, *overall* the relationship must profit both partners—both must be happier for being together.

Many couples resign themselves to experiencing love, and happiness, only in the initial stages of their relationship, but some couples grow closer over time and more deeply in love—because they share meaningful and pleasurable experiences.

◆   ◆   ◆

Like romantic partners, close friends support each other in the attainment of the ultimate currency. Having a close friend to share our lives with—to share the events and thoughts and feelings in our lives—intensifies our experience of meaning, consoles us in our pain, deepens our sense of delight in the world. Intimate friendships, according to seventeenth century philosopher Francis Bacon, "redoubleth joys, and cutteth griefs in half." Without friendship, writes Aristotle, no happiness is possible.

For fifty years, Thomas Jefferson and James Madison worked together to lay the foundation for the new American government. They shared a common purpose and reveled in the pleasure of each other's company. A short time before his death, Jefferson wrote to Madison:

> The friendship which has subsisted between us now half a century and the harmony of our political principles and pursuits have been sources of constant happiness to me through that long period…To myself you have been a pillar of support through life. Take care of me when dead and be assured that I shall leave you with my last affection.

PART III

Meditations on Happiness

First Meditation

Happiness, Self-Interest, and Benevolence

○ ○

Don't ask yourself what the world needs, ask yourself what makes you come alive. And then go and do that. Because what the world needs is people who have come alive.

—*Harold Whitman*

Teaching is my calling. I teach executives in organizations, students in college, and at-risk youth in inner cities. I teach because it makes me happy, because it affords me present and future benefit, pleasure and meaning. I teach because I *want* to (because I love it), not because I feel I *ought* to (out of some abstract sense of duty to others).

In other words, I am no altruist. The ultimate reason that I do anything—whether it is spending time with my friends or doing work for charity—is that it makes me happy. The ultimate currency, in theory and in practice, is the end toward which all of my actions lead.

Some people may feel uncomfortable with the idea that the primary determinant of our actions should be self-interest, our own happiness. The source of such discomfort is a belief—explicit or implicit—in the morality of duty.

Immanuel Kant, arguably the most influential philosopher of the modern era, tells us that for an act to have moral worth, it must be undertaken

69

out of a sense of duty. When we act out of self-interest, then, we preclude the possibility of our action being a moral one. According to Kant, if a person helps another because he feels inclined to do so—because it makes him happy—what he does has no moral value.

Those philosophies and religions that advocate self-sacrifice as the foundation of morality, as Kant does, assume that acting in one's self-interest inevitably leads to acting against the interests of others—that if we do not fight our selfish inclinations, we will sacrifice the lives of others to our own ends.

What this world-view fails to acknowledge, however, is that we do not need to make a choice between helping others and helping ourselves. They are not mutually exclusive possibilities. In fact, as the philosopher Ralph Waldo Emerson explains, "It is one of the most beautiful compensations of this life that no man can sincerely try to help another without helping himself." Helping oneself and helping others are inextricably intertwined: the more we help others the happier we become, and the happier we become, the more inclined we are to help others.

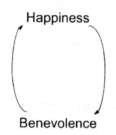

Happiness

Benevolence

Contributing to other people's happiness provides us with meaning and pleasure, which is why helping others is one of the essential components of a happy life. This is not to say that we should live our lives *for* others. If we do not make the pursuit of our own happiness a priority, we are hurting ourselves and, by extension, our inclination to help others. An unhappy person is less likely to be benevolent—and that leads to further unhappiness.

We often enhance our happiness to the greatest extent when we pursue activities that provide us with meaning and pleasure *and* that help others. When making choices, we first need to ask ourselves what would make us happy *independent* of how much it might contribute to the happiness of others. We must then ask ourselves whether what we want to do would deprive others of their ability to pursue their own happiness—because if it would, we would be undermining our happiness. Our empathic inclinations, our innate moral sense, inevitably lead us to pay the price in the ultimate currency when we hurt people.

For those who subscribe to the morality of duty, finding meaning—leading a moral life—necessitates sacrifice. Sacrifice, by definition, is not pleasurable (if it were, it would no longer be sacrifice). The morality of duty, therefore, pits meaning and pleasure against each other.

◆   ◆   ◆

Happiness is not about sacrifice, about a trade-off between present and future benefit, between meaning and pleasure, between helping ourselves and helping others. It is about synthesis, about creating a life in which all of the elements essential to happiness are in harmony.

Second Meditation

Finding Deep Happiness

○ ○

Happiness depends upon ourselves.

—*Aristotle*

Tami, my wife, distinguishes between *height* and *depth* as they relate to happiness: "The height element refers to the fluctuations in our levels of well-being, the highs and lows we experience; the depth of our happiness refers to that part of our well-being that is stable, to our base level of happiness." For example, the sense of relief a rat racer experiences after attaining a goal is transitory; it does not necessarily affect his overall level of happiness. The depth of our happiness is like the roots of a tree—providing the foundation, the constant element of our well-being. The height of our happiness is like the leaves—beautiful, coveted, and yet ephemeral, changing and withering with the seasons.

The question that many philosophers and psychologists have asked is whether the depth of our happiness can be changed or whether we are predestined to experience highs and lows around a fixed level of the ultimate currency.

In his classic work, *Psycho-Cybernetics*, Maxwell Maltz writes about an internal thermostat-like mechanism that controls and checks our happiness level. For most people, the level on which this internal mechanism is set does not change much throughout life—deviations, highs or lows, are quickly corrected and we return to our base level of happiness. Of course,

73

we are delighted when good things happen to us (when, for example, we win a lottery or secure our dream job) and are saddened when things do not go as we would wish (when we lose money or the chance to work at a job we love). These emotions, though, last for only a short time; win or lose, the depth of our happiness does not change and we soon recover our familiar sense of well-being.

The famous Minnesota twin studies, in which identical twins reared apart were shown to have similar personality traits, coupled with research that suggests the existence of a base level of well-being, has led some psychologists to argue that our quota of happiness is determined by our genes or by early experiences—that, as adults, we have no control over how happy we are. The psychologists Lykken and Tellegan, for example, assert that "It may be that trying to be happier is as futile as trying to be taller and is therefore counterproductive."

Such claims, which suggest that our portion of the ultimate currency is predetermined, are misleading. They ignore much evidence that demonstrates that a person's base level of happiness can change. Through therapy, for example, people are able to find happiness that previously eluded them. Some people, through an encounter with a person or by reading a book, following an insight or a realization, have changed their lives for the better.

Psychologists who argue that the depth of our happiness is fixed make the "error of the average"—they derive their conclusions from what most people do while ignoring those who do not fit the norm.[1] Even in the Minnesota twin studies, not all identical twins enjoy identical levels of happiness; in other studies, not all people—100 percent of participants—return to their base level of happiness after each event.

The average is indicative of a trend, not of a necessity or of a universal truth. Often, it is those outside the norm, the exceptional ones, who point

---

[1] A joke I once heard tells of a psychologist who drowned in a pool with an average depth of 10 inches.

to the truth of what is possible. That some people, throughout their lives, enjoy progressively higher levels of happiness indicates that it is possible to re-set the thermostat. The question is, therefore, not whether it is possible, but how. This book provides some, but not all, of the answers. Those who shift their focus from material goods and prestige to the ultimate currency will raise their base level of well-being; those who actively seek present and future benefit will be happier in the long run.

The argument that the depth element of our happiness is immutable is not only misleading, it is also potentially detrimental. A person who is led to believe that, no matter what she does, her share of the ultimate currency is predetermined, is less likely to act and try to better her predicament. Therefore, her belief that her happiness level is fixed and cannot be changed becomes a self-fulfilling prophecy. Worse, the belief that she cannot improve her lot, though predicated on a false theory, might lead her to helplessness and despair.

Some of the questions that we ask ourselves when thinking about the ultimate currency are just as likely to set us up for unhappiness as false theories are. While writing this book or reading others' notions of the good life, when thinking about the ultimate currency and observing the behavior of those around me, I have often asked myself, "Am I happy?" Others, especially those close to me who care about my well-being, have asked me a similar question. It took me a while to recognize that, while well-meaning, this question is not helpful.

How do I determine whether I am happy or not? At what point do I become happy? Is there some universal standard of happiness, and, if so, how do I identify it? Does it depend on my happiness relative to others, and, if so, how do I gauge how happy other people are? There is no reliable way to answer these questions, and even if there were, I would not be happier for it.

"Am I happy?" is a closed question that suggests a binary approach to the pursuit of the ultimate currency: we are either happy or we are not.

Happiness, according to this approach, is an end of a process, a finite and definable point that, when reached, signifies the termination of our pursuit. This point, however, does not exist, and clinging to the belief that it does will lead to dissatisfaction and resignation.

We can always be happier; no person experiences perfect bliss at all times and has nothing more to which he can aspire. Therefore, rather than asking myself whether I am happy or not, a more helpful question is, "How can I become happier?" This question acknowledges the nature of the ultimate currency, and the fact that the pursuit of happiness is an ongoing process that is best represented by an infinite continuum, not by a finite point. Rather than feeling despondent because we have not yet reached the illusive point of perfect happiness, rather than squandering our energies trying to gauge how happy we are, we recognize that there are unlimited resources of happiness and focus on ways in which we can attain more of the ultimate currency.

◆   ◆   ◆

Our pursuit of the ultimate currency can be a never-ending process of flourishing and growth; there is no limit to how much happiness we can attain. By pursuing work, education, and relationships that yield both meaning and pleasure, we become progressively happier—experiencing not just an ephemeral high that withers with the leaves, but lasting happiness with deep and stable roots.

Third Meditation

Preparing for Happiness

○ ○

Most people are about as happy as they make up their minds to be.

—Abraham Lincoln

Our capacity for the pursuit of happiness is a gift of nature. No person, no religion, no ideology, no government has the right to take it away from us. We set up our political structures—our constitutions, our courts of law, our armies—to protect our right to pursue happiness freely. Yet nothing external can protect us from what I have come to believe is the greatest impediment we face in our pursuit of the ultimate currency—our feeling that we are somehow unworthy of happiness.

Understanding the theory of happiness that I have presented here—our need for both pleasure and meaning in our lives—is not enough to guarantee our sustained happiness. If, at some level, we feel unworthy of being happy, we will find ways to limit our capacity for happiness. We may overlook or neglect potential sources of the ultimate currency, we may focus our energy on activities that make us unhappy, we may trivialize the happiness we do experience, or remind ourselves of all the things we are not happy about.

Many people choose to do work they dislike when they could easily find work that would pay them well in the ultimate currency; many people resign themselves to unhappy relationships or to being alone rather than making the effort to find the right people with whom to share their lives. Some people have jobs that provide them present and future benefit, yet still manage to find reasons to be unhappy at work; some people find meaning and pleasure in a relationship, and then find ways to sabotage it. I have done all of these things, and more, to undermine my own happiness.

Why would anyone actively deprive himself of happiness? In her book, *Return to Love*, Marianne Williamson provides insight into this quandary:

> Our deepest fear is not that we are inadequate. Our deepest fear is that we are powerful beyond measure. It is our light, not our darkness, that most frightens us. We ask ourselves who am I to be brilliant, gorgeous, talented and fabulous? Actually, who are you not to be?

Who are we *not* to be happy? Why does the light frighten us more than the darkness? Why do we think that we are unworthy of happiness?

There are external and internal factors, cultural and psychological biases, that conspire against our being happy. On the most fundamental level, the idea that we have the *right* to be happy, that individual happiness is a noble and worthy pursuit, is censured and vilified by many ideologies. Many of the cultural legacies that have been passed down to us presume that we are inherently evil, that we are driven by aggression and the death instinct, that we are born into original sin—that our lives unredeemed by the civilizing forces of our culture would be, in the words of the philosopher Thomas Hobbes, "solitary, poor, nasty, brutish, and short." Who would deem these creatures deserving of happiness? With such views so deeply ingrained in our culture, it is no wonder we feel ourselves more suited to the darkness than the light.

The pervasiveness of these views makes them almost invisible to us; we become desensitized to their presence because they have formed our assumptions about how much happiness we are capable or worthy of. Becoming more aware of the ways in which such assumptions limit us can help us to transform, for instance, the idea of original sin (that we are born bad and hence unworthy of happiness) into the idea of *original virtue* (that we are born good and hence worthy of happiness). If we believe in original virtue, we are more likely to accept our birthright to pursue happiness.

The assumptions that hold us back are not only the ones we have internalized from our predecessors. Many of us have limitations that are self-generated. For example, when we do not feel that we are worthy of happiness we cannot possibly feel worthy of the good things in our lives, the things that bring us happiness. Because we do not believe we actually deserve them, that they could really be ours, we fear their loss. This fear causes actual behaviors that lead to a self-fulfilling prophecy: our fear of loss creates actual loss, our feelings of being unworthy of happiness in fact lead to unhappiness.

A person who fears loss may protect himself by ensuring that he has nothing to lose. When we are happy we have a lot to lose. To avoid the devastation of a loss we exclude the possibility of any gain. We fear the worst and thus, from the outset, deprive ourselves of the best.

Even if we do find happiness, we might feel guilty because there are other people who are less fortunate. The implicit, and false, assumption underlying such sentiments is that happiness is a zero-sum-game—that one person's happiness (our own) necessarily deprives others of theirs. But as Williamson points out, "As we let our light shine, we unconsciously give other people permission to do the same. As we are liberated from our own fear, our presence automatically liberates others." It is when we liberate ourselves from our fear of happiness that we can best help others.

To lead a happy life we must also experience a sense of *metaphysical worthiness*.[1] As Nathaniel Branden writes, "In order to seek values, man must consider himself worthy of enjoying them. In order to fight for his happiness, he must consider himself worthy of happiness." We must

---

1.   Meta-physical means "above" the physical, that which transcends the physical. In this context, metaphysical refers to our intangible qualities and characteristics.

appreciate our core self, who we really are, independent of our tangible accomplishments; we must believe that we deserve to be happy; we must feel that we are worthy by *virtue* of our existence—because we are born with the heart and mind to experience pleasure and meaning.

When we do not accept our metaphysical worth, we ignore or actively undermine our talents, our potential, our joy, our accomplishments. For example, we might employ the "yes, but..." technique: *Yes*, I do have meaning and pleasure in my life, *but* what if it doesn't last? *Yes*, I love my job, *but* what if I get bored as I often do? *Yes*, I have found a partner I love, *but* what if she leaves me? Refusing to accept the good things that happen to us leads to unhappiness and, given that we are still unhappy despite all the potential sources of happiness in our lives, to resignation.

◆   ◆   ◆

Before we are able to receive a gift, from a friend or from nature, we have to be open to it; a bottle with its cap screwed on tightly cannot be filled with water no matter how much water we try to pour into it or how often we try—the water simply runs down its sides, never filling it. Metaphysical worthiness is a state of openness—of being open to happiness.

Fourth Meditation

Imagining Happiness

○ ○

Life would be infinitely happier if we could only be born at the age of eighty and gradually approach eighteen.

—Mark Twain

You are eighty years old. A time machine has just been invented and you are selected as one of the first people to use it. The inventor, a scientist from NASA, tells you that you will be transported back to the day when, as it happens, you first read *The Question of Happiness*. You, with the wisdom of having lived and experienced life, have fifteen minutes to spend with your young and inexperienced self. What do you say when you meet? What advice do you give yourself?

I formulated this thought experiment after reading an account by Psychiatrist Irvin Yalom of terminally ill cancer patients. Yalom describes how

> an open confrontation with death allows many patients to move into a mode of existence that is richer than the one they experienced prior to their illness. Many patients report dramatic shifts in life perspective. They are able to trivialize the trivial, to assume a sense of control, to stop doing things they do not wish to do, to communicate more openly with families and close friends, and to live entirely in the present rather

than in the future or the past...As one's focus turns from the trivial diversions of life, a fuller appreciation of the elemental factors in existence may emerge: the changing seasons, the falling leaves, the last spring, and especially, the loving of others. Over and over we hear our patients say..."Why did we have to wait until now, till we are riddled with cancer, to learn how to value and appreciate life?"

What struck me about Yalom's and others' accounts of people finding themselves—beginning to live life fully, for the first time—is that following the news of their terminal disease, they were still the same people with the same knowledge of life's questions and answers, the same cognitive and emotional capacities. No one descended from Mount Sinai presenting them with commandments on how to live; no Greek sage or oracle revealed to them the secrets to the good life; no one injected them with mind or heart enhancing drugs; they did not discover a new and revolutionary self-help book that changed their lives.

Yet, with the capacities they have always had—which seemed to be inadequate in making them happy before—their lives changed. They gained no new knowledge, but, rather, an acute awareness of what they knew all along. In other words, they had within them the knowledge of how they should live life. It was just that they ignored this knowledge, or were not conscious of it.

What the time travel thought experiment does is make us aware of life's brevity, and preciousness. Granted, an eighty-year-old has more experience—and there are no shortcuts in terms of gaining much of the knowledge that a full life can give us—but some of what we become aware of when we are eighty we already know when we are twenty. It is a matter of awareness. To paraphrase Oscar Wilde, youth does not necessarily need to be wasted on the young.

◆   ◆   ◆

There is very little that any philosophy, psychology, or self-help book can teach us that is new about attaining the ultimate currency. Often, a book or a teacher can do no more than help us raise our levels of awareness, become cognizant of what we already know. Ultimately, our progress, our growth, and our happiness come from our ability to look within ourselves and ask the important questions—and, especially, the question of questions.

Conclusion

What Now?

Be the change you want to see in the world.

—Gandhi

I am optimistic about the possibility of change toward a more emotionally prosperous society. I believe that people can find work that will provide them present and future benefit, that people can find education a rich source of the ultimate currency, that people can find meaningful and pleasurable relationships. I do not, however, believe that these changes will happen overnight.

In this book I present a neat and structured theory of happiness, but life is neither neat nor structured. A theory, at best, can establish a stable Archimedean point amid the flux of life, a platform from which we can ask the right questions. Of course, making the transition from theory to practice is difficult: changing deeply-rooted habits of thinking, transforming ourselves and our world, requires a great deal of effort.

People often abandon theories when they discover how difficult it is to put them into practice. It seems odd that most of us are prepared to work extremely hard for quantifiable ends, yet give up quickly when it comes to pursuing the ultimate currency. If we want to find happiness we must commit ourselves to working hard at it, for while there is one easy step to *un*happiness—doing nothing—there are no easy steps to happiness.

Yet even if we commit ourselves to working hard, the path to happiness is never free of obstacles. How can a single mother with three children to support think of leaving her mundane but well-paying job for a more meaningful occupation? How can the millions of people who were taught that the ultimate currency is money and prestige reconstruct their value system and begin to pursue the *real* ultimate currency?

Within the parameters of each life, it is usually possible to introduce happiness boosters, activities that will provide both meaning and pleasure. Change often comes incrementally, in small doses. The single mother can begin by taking a class one night a week. A rat racer who feels stuck and unhappy can begin by devoting a little extra time to his family. One small change can have significant consequences: a single candle can light up a dark room.

If Not Now, Then When

My friend Kim and I walked around Provincetown, admiring the quaint shops on the main street, listening to the waves breaking on the rocks, breathing in the salty air, savoring that precious feeling of being outside of time that can come when one is in a small town on vacation.

At the time, I was a graduate student living in the competitive environment of the university. I told Kim that as soon as I graduated, I wanted to move to a place like Provincetown. I thought that without the looming deadlines and the deadly pace, I would finally experience the calm I had been looking for my entire life. I had often thought about moving to a quiet place after graduation, but as the idea took on the form of words—became tangible—I felt uneasy.

Had I not just fallen into the trap of living in the future? Did I really have to wait until graduation? Kim and I had been working on this book together, and were talking and thinking a lot about the question of happiness. We had been talking about how, despite being in a competitive environment, with a great deal of work, keeping a fast pace, we could still experience calm. Kim said, "The calmness has to be inside. If you're happy, that happiness is transportable—you take it with you wherever you go." She paused and then added, "Not that the external isn't significant, but it doesn't *make* us happy."

We often imagine that when we reach some future destination, we will feel accomplished, calm, and ready for happiness. We tell ourselves that, with the attainment of certain goals, we will finally find peace. We tell ourselves that this will happen once we graduate from college, or get tenure, or make enough money, or have a family and children, or—reach any other number of goals which will likely change over the course of our lives. Yet in most cases, shortly after reaching some destination, we return to our base level of well-being. If we are normally anxious and stressed, those feelings will likely return soon after reaching a goal we thought would change our lives.

Much of the rat racer's tension stems from the need to feel control over the future. As a result, she lives in the future. The rat racer lives by the "what *if*" rather than by the "what *is*"—in the tense hypothetical future rather than in the calm real present. What if I don't do well on the exam? What if I don't get a promotion? What if I can't afford the mortgage on my new house? Rather than fully experiencing the here and now, she is, in the words of poet Galway Kinnell, "smearing the darkness of expectation across experience."

Then there are those who, stuck in the past, do not allow themselves to experience happiness in the present. They rehearse their unsatisfying histories, their attempts to live first as rat racers, then as hedonists; they brood over the relationships they tried to rekindle to no avail, the many jobs they worked at without finding their true calling. Always reliving the past, concerned with justifying their unhappiness, they forgo the potential for happiness in their lives.

Rather than allowing ourselves to remain enslaved by our past or future, we must work to realize, to make real, our birthright—the day-to-day pursuit of a life of pleasure and meaning, a life in which we luxuriate in the fullness of feeling that happiness brings.

◆   ◆   ◆

You have a choice. You have a choice now, and at every moment in your life, to pursue the ultimate currency.

About the Author

Tal Ben-Shahar graduated from Harvard University with a degree in Philosophy and Psychology. He was an internationally ranked squash player, Israeli national champion, US intercollegiate champion, and All-American. For the last ten years, Tal has been teaching personal and organizational excellence, leadership, ethics, and self-esteem. His experience spans from leadership workshops for at-risk youth to consulting and conducting seminars for senior executives in multinational corporations. Tal writes and publishes extensively on various topics—education, philosophy, politics, psychology, and art. For more information about his work see **www.ReflAction.org.**

References

Boldt, L. G. (1999). *Zen and the Art of Making a Living: A Practical Guide to Creative Career Design.* Penguin.

Bronner, E. (1998). College Freshmen Aiming for High Marks in Income. *New York Times.*

Branden, N. In Ayn Rand's (1989). *The Virtue of Selfishness.* New American Library.

Branden, N. (1994). *The Six Pillars of Self-Esteem.* Bantam Books.

Brickman, P. Coates, D., & Bulman R. J. (1978). Lottery winners and accidents victims: Is happiness relative? *Journal of Personality and Social Psychology,* 36: 917-27.

Buckingham M., & Clifton, D. O. (2001). *Now, Discover Your Strengths.* Free Press.

Collins, M. (1992). *Ordinary Children, Extraordinary Teachers.* Hampton Roads.

Coopersmith, S. (1967). *The Antecedents of Self-Esteem.* Freeman.

Csikszentmihalyi, M. (1998). *Finding Flow: The Psychology of Engagement With Everyday Life.* Basic Books.

Csikszentmihalyi, M., & Lefevre, J. (1989). Optimal experience in work and leisure. *Journal of Personality and Social Psychology,* 56, 815-822.

Damasio, A. R. (1995). *Descartes' Error: Emotion, Reason and the Human Brain.* Avon Books.

Diener, E., Suh, E. M., Lucas, R. E., & Smith, H. L. (1999). Subjective well-being: Three decades of progress. *Psychological Bulletin*, 125: 276-302.

Gilbert, D. T., Pinel, E. C., Wilson, T. D., Blumberg, S. J., & Wheatley, T. P. (1998). Immune neglect: A source of durability bias in affective forecasting. *Journal of Personality and Social Psychology*, 75: 617-638.

Ginott, H. G. (1995). *Teacher and Child: A Book for Parents and Teachers*. Collier Books.

Goleman, D. (1995). *Emotional Intelligence*. Bantam Books.

Hatfield, E., Traupmann, J., Sprecher, S., Utne, M., & Hay, J. (1985). Equity and Intimate Relations: Recent Research. In W. Ickes (Ed.), *Compatible and Incompatible Relationships*. Springer-Verlag.

Kant, I. (1985). *Foundations of the Metaphysics of Morals*. Translated by L. W. Beck. Macmillan Publishing Company.

Lillard, P. P. (1996) . *Montessori Today: A Comprehensive Approach to Education from Birth to Adulthood*. Schocken Books.

Lykken, D., & Tellegen, A. (1996). Happiness is a stochastic phenomenon. *Psychological Science, 7,* 186–189.

Maslow, A. H. (1993). *The Farther Reaches of Human Nature*. Arkana.

Maltz, M. (1960). *Psycho-Cybernatics*. Pocket Books.

Nozick, R. (1989). *The Examined Life: Philosophical Meditations*. Simon & Schuster.

Pirsig, R. M. (1984). *Zen and the Art of Motorcycle Maintenance: An Inquiry into Values*. Bantam Books.

Seligman, M. E. P. (1990). *Learned Optimism: How to Change Your Mind and Your Life*. Pocket Books.

Smiles, S. (1958). *Self-Help*. John Murray.

Williamson, M. (1996). *Return to Love: Reflections on the Principles of a Course in Miracles*. Harper Collins.

Yalom, I. D. (1998). *The Yalom Reader: Selections from the Work of a Master Therapist and Storyteller*. Edited by B. Yalom. Basic Books.

0-595-23140-3

Printed in the United States
60563LVS00004B/538-567